Arabian Son

21 Stories

Tim Barger

Selwa 🌴 Press

All rights are reserved. No part of this work may be used or reproduced in any manner or form without written permission from the publisher. Fair use, defined as 200 words or less, is permitted for use in reviews or commentary.

ISBN: 978-0-98820505-5

Copyright © 2014 Timothy J. Barger

Published by Selwa Press
SelwaDigital.com / SelwaPress.com
Queries: Editor@SelwaPress.com

Made in the USA

Tim & Mike Barger - 1958

To Smith, Milt and Lana.
Most especially to my co-conspirator.

Daphne,
Hope that you enjoy the stories. Thanks for all your help over the years.

Tim

Janet Norma Harryman - Les Snyder 1940

INTRODUCTION

I'm not sure who was the first American born in Arabia, but I do know that in 1940 Janet Norma Harryman was the second child and the first American girl born in Dhahran. Seven years later I became the seventh Aramco baby. Janet and I were the beginning of an exclusive demographic, a members-only club, that today numbers into the many thousands.

Until 1956 we were all born in one of two maternity beds in the first hospital. The building subsequently became the Women's Exchange, a community resale shop operated by the Dhahran Women's Group. Reading these stories you can well imagine how my mother used to daydream about taking me back to exchange for a Waring blender.

Americans born in an isolated oil camp surrounded by miles of desert weren't Saudi citizens, yet we weren't entirely Americans either – the United States was a country we briefly visited every two years. We knew America only from the newsreels, year-old movies and the books and magazines we read.

In a time when air travel was exclusive because it was extremely expensive, As teenagers we blithely flew around Europe with our Aramco bags in hand. We were more comfortable in Beirut or Rome than we were in Houston or Los Angeles but the cities we really knew were oil camps. Abqaiq, Dhahran or Ras Tanura, the towns of Aramco, shaped all of us as children, and to this day we cherish the backyards, alleys and street corners where our lives unfolded..

With all the Saudis of the Eastern Province, we shared the elemental beauty of the desert, the inky night sky and the blue-green waters of the Gulf. The searing-hot summer afternoons, the fury of the spring shamaals, the pervasive fog-like humidity, cool, clear winter nights splattered with bright stars like they were painted with celestial spray-paint. The blazing streaks of phosphorescence that lit the water of Half Moon Bay with brilliant neon amazed and delighted everyone regardless of which language they spoke. All of these phenomena influenced us so deeply that in many ways we had more in common with the Saudis than we did with our own culture.

So in the end, I guess Janet Norma and I are part of an exclusive clan of Aramco-Americans born or raised in

Arabia. I wrote these stories for us. Most take place before the mid-60s but I'm fairly certain that later generations will recognize many of the venues and landmarks as well as the near-anarchic sense of adventure that made growing up in Dhahran such a glorious privilege.

Tim Barger

CONTENTS

Introduction	6
Hooky	13
Hidden Places	22
Scott Miller's Invention	25
Rites of Passage	27
Playing Cards	32
The Gingerbread Boy	35
First Steps	39
Dhahran's Palace of Dreams	41
Think Ahead	48
Looking for Lana	56
Walking to Ras Tanura	63
The Swim Meet	66
Tequila!	74
Higher Learning	78
The Secret Door	83
Kangaroo Bikes	91
Abu Hamid	100
Special Techniques	105
The Double-Shot Solution	112
Welcome to Riyadh	115
The Rule of Life	123

Tim Barger 7, David Snyder 9, and Mary Barger age 3.

HOOKY

For some unknown reason, throughout my life various circumstances have led me into unusual situations. Perhaps the drummer I was marching to played Stockhausen on the snares but these predicaments began early in life. I was born in Dhahran in 1947 where I lived on 11th street. Hamilton House, the palatial, by Dhahran standards, company guest house was on the next block to the north. It was the only place with a lawn-covered hill in town. Rolling down the slope was great fun, and you'd always come home with grass-stained jeans, itching like mad from the bugs in the grass.

To the south was the block closest to recreation, on the large median between our blocks were two bachelorette portables anchored at the bottom of the sloping road with a gorgeous wood-slatted central air conditioning plant. The bachelorette portables were terrific. If you were a kid, you could knock on the door and almost always some lovely single woman would answer, invite you in and spoil you with cookies and maybe a Pepsi. A block further on was the recreation complex: the pool, the bowling alley, the Fiesta Room – a snack bar and coffee shop – the tennis courts, the ball field, the movie theater and, unfortunately, the school.

I didn't really have anything against school. My brother and sister went there. But it did seem somewhat constricting as you had to go every day at the same time. So when I turned 6, it was off to the Gulag. However my family was on a short leave, so I started Kindergarten a week or so late.

At that time Kindergarten was held in a portable adjacent to the pool that later achieved infamy as the Teen Canteen. I showed up and was amazed to find all these kids I didn't know running around before class. Dhahran was small but my circle of acquaintances was even smaller. I wasn't there long that day before I noticed the cutest girl with jet-black hair cut in a pageboy. The other boys noticed her too, called out her name, Stephanie, and chased her and her friends around the play area. Of course, when Stephanie stopped, the boys froze and didn't know what to do next. The girls would laugh and scurry off to be chased some more.

In the middle of all this confusion we heard someone yelling, "Help! Help!" from the pool area. A dozen or more of us poured through the picket fence gate to see someone that I knew - hollering helplessly, upside down in a tree.

It was Jimmy R. He had been climbing a young ficus tree about 10 feet tall, had slipped and was suspended 4 feet from the ground by his ankle caught in the crook of a branch. He was red-faced, screaming in terror. Like a band of munchkins, we swarmed around him with not the slightest idea how to save him. After a minute or two, Sebastian, the big Goanese lifeguard, strode in like King Kong, grabbed Jimmy's ankle and plucked him out of the tree like it was the simplest thing in the world. We were amazed and all crowded around to congratulate him for his escape from an untimely death.

After the melee subsided a bit, I was talking to Jimmy when Stephanie appeared to ask if he was okay. He talked to her for a minute and then in a moment of humanity and compassion that I'll always cherish him for, he introduced her to me. She smiled at me with dancing eyes and said, "So nice to meet you, sir," and then laughed and bounded off. I didn't know if she was joking or being sincere or what. I didn't care. I was in heaven. Now she knew my name, "Sir."

The bell rang, and we all marched into class. Everyone but me seemed to know what they were supposed to do but I bumbled along and the teacher told me that I was to bring a rug the next day for Nap Time. Looking back I can imagine that the teacher couldn't wait every day until she could call for Nap Time.

So on my second day of Kindergarten I trooped off to school but for some reason I was late. When I got to the portable, the door was closed and class had already started. I sort of panicked. If I went in now, everyone would laugh at me. Not so bad but what would Stephanie think about me? After about 30 seconds of careful deliberation and deep soul searching, I dumped my rug and fled. Thus began my descent into a life of criminality, a desperate fugitive on the run.

I didn't know exactly where to go but ended up on the bit of the rocky jebal that remained behind the fenced patio of the Kindergarten portable, next to the hobby shop. There was some unspoiled ground there with a gnarled acacia tree on the slope. I sat under the tree and watched lizards doing push-ups in the heat. Satisfied that blood hounds had not been unleashed on my trail, I circled around behind the bowling alley and made my way to the library.

At that time the library was situated above the Fiesta Room. It wasn't a really big space but was crammed with bookshelves and presided over by two very good-natured Indian librarians. They recognized me from past visits and it never occurred to them that I should be in school. I couldn't read, but on the bottom shelf for oversized books there were dozens of volumes of cartoon books. I especially remember the cartoon annuals from The New Yorker. Aramco must have had every edition from 1940 on. So I sat on the floor and ate it up. You didn't have to read to enjoy the cartoons, and that is probably where I began a life-long addiction to desert island and "take me to your leader" cartoons. If I got stuck, one of those Indian librarians would be happy to read me the captions.

After a few hours of cartoons I'd get restless and roam around the camp. Along the perimeter fence it was still pretty much desert. Walking along the chain link fence I was always attracted to the fly traps placed intermittently along the length. They were painted bright red with warning signs stenciled on the side, but you could smell them way before you could read the warning, if you could read. They smelled god-awful but how could you resist getting as close to them as possible without throwing up and wondering what horrible brew they contained? How could something that smelled that terrible attract anything, even flies?

Of course the fence wasn't exactly perfect. Walking along you could find places where jackals and feral dogs had burrowed underneath it. So I'd wiggle under the chain link and be in the official desert. In those days Dhahran was completely surrounded by desert. You could walk from camp all the way to the Persian Gulf without seeing a fence, a wall, a road, a house or anything but sand and rock.

Nowadays Dhahran is part of a sprawling megalopolis that extends to Khobar and the Gulf. There isn't a square yard that isn't developed. But back then, I'd putter around for a while, living it up in the knowledge that I was free in the wild, slightly puzzled because the desert on this side didn't look any different than the desert behind the fence.

By some sixth sense I always knew when Kindergarten was over. I'd show up in time to meet the other kids coming home from school and ask them what they did that day. When I got home, my mother would ask me what I did in school that day. I'd mumble something about playing with blocks or reciting the colors of the rainbow or whatever. I quickly learned that if I burst in the door and said, "We sang Old MacDonald today," that was plenty enough information and I could escape into the backyard to hunt for caterpillars in the hedge or play with my small militia of plastic soldiers and steel Dinky toy trucks in the soft dirt dirt.

This went on for days and then weeks, until I had convinced myself that, "Yes, I was going to school every day" – just in a different classroom. No one else in Kindergarten was doing advanced arithmetic such as fractions but I was doing them every day. The refund on a Pepsi bottle was a quarter-riyal and a Pepsi was a riyal. It was easy to scrounge through a few alleys to find four empty bottles. The hard part was getting the refund at the commissary. The place was swarming with moms, and if my mother's friends – or worse, my mother – saw me, I was sunk.

Once I was sure the coast was clear, I'd sneak into the commissary, get my refund, buy my Pepsi and hot-foot it out of there, slinking behind the Mail Center to the Barber Shop. Another portable building raised about 6 feet high, it had a wooden staircase up from the sidewalk where I could crawl under the stairs and sip my warm Pepsi in shade and perfect safety. It's funny that looking out, all that I could see were people from the knee down which fittingly reminded me of the Tom and Jerry cartoons where adults were always seen only as legs walking in and out of the frame. When I was finished, I'd stash the bottle and know that I only needed three-quarters of a riyal to get my next fix. I was a whiz with fractions.

A lot of times I'd hang with the gardeners. They were an odd group of people because they just appeared out of nowhere, completely unofficial. I don't know how they got past the main gate into camp, where they lived or even who paid them. They were just there. I'd find a guy working in someone's back yard and just hang around.

In retrospect, I imagine most of the gardeners were semi-indentured agriculture workers from Qatif or Hofuf, but to me at the time they were just cheerful men in once-white undershirts with white head-dresses and wrap-around waist sarongs. They mostly wore sandals but some of them wore sort of virtual sandals, cheap shoes with the backs crushed down so you could slip into them.

Every gardener seemed to have only two tools: a hoe and a hand scythe. A crescent shaped blade about a foot long with a wooden handle, the wicked-looking hand scythe was of particular interest. The gardeners used it to trim hedges, cut back branches and even mow lawns. They'd let me use it and show me how to handle the thing, but I was too little to wield it effectively and even then came to appreciate how strong you had to be to use it all day long.

Occasionally a gardener would take a break and invite me to share from his lunch pail. In those days most of the Saudi workers had a cylinder-shaped, aluminum lunch pail that was segmented into three sections that nestled into each other with a handle that locked the parts together. The top section held their Arab bread called *khubz*, the second section was for gravy or sauce and the much larger bottom section packed the rice. I usually just had a few nibbles of the *khubz* as we sat together in the shade chatting back and forth. I say chatting but I have no idea how we communicated save through sign language and various expressions and gestures.

At the time I only knew a few Arabic words. *Na'am* meant "yes," *La* meant "no," *Wajid zain* meant "very good" and *Kaaf halaak* meant "how are you?" Shortly thereafter I learned that indispensable and always useful phrase, *Inta simak wajeh* which means "You are a fish face." Nonetheless we got along famously.

One day a gardener and I were in an alley behind some houses that were situated much higher than the alley level, so the company had built a high, stone retaining wall and back filled the void to make the back yard level. The gardener pointed to a clay drainage pipe set in the wall. He motioned for me to put my hand into the pipe. I stuck my hand in and felt drifted fine sand. I wiggled my fingers around until I felt some small, smooth objects. I pulled out my hand and placed into my palm three lizard eggs that glistened like pearls. Perfectly spherical, white as fine alabaster, they seemed to glow in my hand as I rolled them around, mesmerized by their simple beauty.

After a minute the gardener gestured for me to put them back in the pipe. For many years after that, heedless of the possibility of vipers, scorpions or spiders, I thrust my hand into countless pipes lying abandoned around the outskirts of camp in search of those precious lizard eggs.

Dhahran was still being built in those days, and I discovered the Saudi work crews finishing houses on what I'm guessing was about Ninth Street. All about, there was a flurry of activity, plumbers and painters, roofers laying down shingles and plasterers slathering stucco over the lathe. This was some real action. Initially the crews ignored me but after a while they warmed up, offered me dates and mocked each other in pantomime just so I would laugh. I'm sure that I was more of a novelty to them than they were to me.

They noticed that when an American supervisor would appear I would make myself scarce until he left. Eventually they warned me when the big boss was approaching. My second day on the job site, a plasterer took me aside and using some plaster on a shingle switly shaped a fish and then deftly transformed it into a bird as if he were some primitive Saudi Picasso.

Again I'm not sure how we communicated but he told me that if I came the next day he would show me how to make a bird trap out of a piece of garden hose. There couldn't be anything much better than that, so I went home high on the next day's prospects. I opened the door to my house to be greeted by my mom's voice from the living room, "Timothy. Is that you?" She only used my full name when I was in trouble, so I knew I was doomed.

My teacher had spotted my sister Annie at school and said, "Oh, are you back from vacation?" It turned out that, without even meaning to, I had set the world's record for truancy in the Dhahran school system grades K through nine. I had played hooky for a month.

My mother Kathleen was so angry that she could barely speak but she managed. Basically I was grounded for my entire life just after she introduced me to Mr. Hairbrush.

When my dad came home from work, he wasn't too amused either. I got another tongue lashing and a few raps on the head with his knuckles. I was sent to bed without dinner too. All in all, it wasn't the most successful day but what really bothered me was that I was never going to learn how to make that bird trap out of a garden hose.

The next day my mother escorted me to class. The same kids were milling around but to my great dismay Stephanie wasn't there. Her dad had been transferred to Abqaiq where she reigned for many years as one of the prettiest girls in a town overflowing with pretty girls. She still is beautiful. I see her once in a while at reunions and can't help but remember that day when she called me "Sir."

This whole remembrance was triggered one day when I was at my daughter's house and my bright-eyed granddaughter Beatrice arrived home from kindergarten. Looking at her, I was struck by just how very short 6-year-old kids are.

My daughter would have an apoplectic seizure if Bea were unsupervised for an hour, let alone a month.

My mother wasn't mad at me; she was out of her mind with worry about what terrible things might have happened to me while wandering around on my own. She really shouldn't have been worried. I wasn't. Because somehow I knew that Dhahran in the 50s was probably the safest place on earth.

Ras Tanura Tennis Courts / Theater - Wallie Ballor 1946

HIDDEN PLACES

As kids growing up in Dhahran in the 50s, we were naturally attracted to alleys and rat holes and hidden places totally devoid of adult supervision. One neat but prosaic place was inside the tepee-like hedge that anchored Christmas Tree circle. You could go through a small door at the bottom and hang around within, maybe smoking a stolen cigarette or just laughing at some inanity or another. However, it was very popular and far from secret. Even the very little kids knew about it.

The first recreational place Aramco built was the tennis courts, probably in the mid-30s. They put a fence of plaited palm fronds around them to keep out the wind, and it made a good place to show the outdoor movies. They planted a hedge around the fence and added water. The fence grew taller as did the hedge. By the mid-50s the fence, now made of chain-link, and the hedge were maybe 25 or 30 feet high.

Prowling around one day looking for something to do, one of us noticed that there was a narrow space between the fence and the hedge. So with some difficulty we wiggled between and started climbing up. It wasn't exactly simple because in many places the hedge and the fence were completely entangled. Also the hedge was filthy with years of accumulated dirt, DDT and Malathion. Eventually we were dusted from hedge to toe with the stuff. But it was all worth it when we got to the top.

We emerged at the top of the hedge, 30 feet off the ground. Then we crawled out on the tangle of branches to perch like some kind of strange birds nesting. We could see everything from the school to the pool, the patio, the bowling alley, all the way to the theater. Way up in the air, we watched people come and go – the gardeners working on the ball field, the bachelors and bachelorettes flirting with each other en route to the Fiesta Room, mothers hurrying their children to the swimming pool, cars driving down King's Road.

We could see them but, because they had not the slightest inclination to look up, they couldn't see us. Like mocking birds we mocked and laughed, high above the world as we knew it.

Looking south at Hamilton House on 11th Street - H.K.Beckley 1948

SCOTT MILLER'S INVENTION

Eight year-olds in the mid-1950s, we roamed Dhahran like feral animals on bicycles in search of even the slightest diversion. One day we landed at Scott Miller's house on Christmas Tree Circle to behold his new invention, a long piece of rope tied to the handle on the metal lid of one of those Aramco-issue garbage cans with the other end knotted firmly to the stem of his bicycle seat. As if he had discovered fire, Scott glowed like Prometheus with the satisfaction of his ingenuity as he demonstrated its brilliance.

Riding around the circle, he dragged the screeching lid and was able to make it perform like a water skier who first swings widely to the right and then quickly to the opposite side of the arc. We jumped with delight when it first crashed into the tire of a parked car and then bounced back out from the rubber bumper. And again when it came screeching back into the tire of the next car and rebounded wildly. He did the whole circle, maybe half a dozen cars, and we howled in approval.

Feeding on our joy, he redoubled his speed and circled again. Working one car after another, he sailed the galvanized disk to and fro, each ricochet fueling the speed of the next to come. Wild-eyed with manic glee, he grinned at us over his shoulder. The thin, flying puck skittered towards the next target ... and wedged itself firmly behind the tire. The rope tightened, and his bike came to an instant halt. Scott didn't.

With the most wonderful expression of surprise and self-realized irony Scott Miller sailed over the handlebars and into mythology. He hit the street face-first, bounced along the hot asphalt and slammed into the curb. We were all stunned into silence – for about ten seconds – then erupted in convulsions of laughter. It was so hysterical that each of us died a thousand deaths, mirthful witnesses to a sublime miracle of humor, a gift from the goddess of Fun to her devotees.

Mr. Whipple's class. Left to right, circled: Scott Miller, Maco and Tim

RITES OF PASSAGE

In the Dhahran of the 50s there were many rites of passage. For instance, the involuntary type like when you are perfectly content riding your bicycle down the street and a fly shoots into your open mouth and down your throat. You crash your bike to the asphalt, coughing and choking, certain that you are about to die.

Or there is the voluntary kind such as the first time you jump off the end of the salt water injection pier at Abqaiq beach or when you slip out of camp at night, head for the jebal and climb to the top of the radio tower. Spread out below you is all of Dhahran, bathed in the flickering glow of the flares at the Stabilizer, the night sky littered with stars like so many rhinestones strewn on black velvet. What a view.

Billy James who lived across the street was an eighth-grader, four years older than me but sometimes he let me hang around. One day he told me that there was a labyrinth of tunnels that stretched endlessly beneath the movie theater. They were dark and pitiless, teeming with fanged albino rats, venomous snakes and tarantulas as big as your fist. You had to be careful as one wrong turn and you'd be lost, doomed to die of hunger beneath the movies. How could I resist?

The next week the strike team assembled for Pepsi at the Fiesta Room, me and Maco and the famous Scott Miller. We reviewed our equipment: Maco had a flashlight, Scott had one of those aluminum Army-style canteens and I had a ball of red yarn so we wouldn't get lost, we also had three Mars bars just in case.

All checked off, we nonchalantly strolled out the door, turned left past the recreation office and the theater, quickly turned left again at the corner and instantly became furtive, even though there wasn't a soul to see us. About halfway down the side of the theater against the wall was a large, square concrete-block well about 8 feet deep where the grates for the ventilation system waited.

We crawled down to the grating, lifted up a section and dropped in. Yawning before us was the gaping maw of the main air conditioning outlet duct. I tied off the yarn and we climbed in. The cross section of the sheet metal ducting was maybe 3 feet high and 4 feet wide, not exactly roomy. The first thing we noticed once we were in was that the ducting flexed back and forth making a helluva thunder-like sound. So we tried to creep slowly without setting it off.

After about 15 feet we ran out of yarn. Oh well. We pressed on through a thick layer of lint, dust, stray asbestos insulation and god knows what else. The theater was built in 1947, so at least ten years of filmy debris was stirred into the air. After another few feet Maco dropped the flashlight with a loud bang that echoed up and down the duct. The light didn't work after that unless you hit it and then it would only flicker a bit and go off. There was still some light from the opening so we kept on – still no fanged rats – until the duct turned 90 degrees. We looked around the corner and could see some light and hear a little noise. Famished by then, we ate the Mars bars. We continued on for a bit until Scott opened the canteen for a drink and dropped it. It clunked against the sheet metal, reverberating like a sonic boom, then gurgled away in the dark. Now we were mucking through linty mud, but the sound only got louder.

Finally we wiggled forward to reach the wide grating where the duct, hidden under the stage, sucked air out of the theater. We made our way up to the grill work and could see everybody on the other side raptly watching the movie. All the front row seats were occupied by kids we knew, the reflected light from the screen flickering across them in different colors and shades, the soundtrack blaring. They didn't know that we were there, just 10 feet away. Cheryl DiGiacomo, Lynn Tietjen, Diane Sherman and Gayle Miller sitting quietly together. Tom Moss and Ron Poole sprawled out like pashas. Twila Jones and

Barbara Hassan eating popcorn. Tommy Williams, Doug Tedsen and Hammond jabbing each other in the ribs. Donna Gibson and Mary Catherine Teal sharing some smuggled French fries. Ralph Wells twitching in the end seat.

We were mesmerized. As stupid and as insensitive as we were, we realized that this was a magic moment: The shifting light across their faces, the disembodied sound booming away, the cool air blowing past us.

A roar echoed through the ducting and broke the spell. "You boys, come out of there, right now!" Busted.

"You're in big trouble. Right now!"

Resigned to our fate, we crawled back out, through the mud of the spilled canteen, past the Mars bar wrappers, to the end of the red yarn and out to the opening where Sebastian, the Goanese lifeguard, scowled at us. Behind his game face he was probably howling with laughter at the sight of us covered with mud, our hair powdered with lint, asbestos and dust. He took us to the Recreation Office where some American dressed us down and sent us home. The next day our parents received notices that we were banned from the entire recreation block for a week.

Four days later – it seemed like a month to us – we sneaked through the bowling alley door into the kids' side of the Fiesta Room where we regaled a rapt audience about our adventure: the albino rats with bloody fangs, the viper that Scott crushed with his canteen, the enormous scorpion that struck at my sneaker and left his stinger attached and the huge cobweb like cotton candy that nearly suffocated Maco. Swear to God. It was terrible. We don't know how we made it out alive.

And undoubtedly some kid in the room that day began making his own plans to enter the labyrinth of certain death.

PLAYING CARDS

In fifth grade there was a kid I'll call Cecil. A clumsy, good natured guy with a great goofy smile, he was big as a ninth-grader, but not the shiniest spoon on the table. One night while his parents were at a party he decided to poke around in his dad's top drawer. After a bit of browsing around … Bingo! A deck of nudie playing cards. After going through them carefully, he figured he could pocket a few and his dad would never notice. Not sharp thinking because when his dad found the queen of hearts, the black deuce and the jack of diamonds gone, Cecil's days would be numbered. But that was for another time.

The next morning, Cecil showed up at school and became the most popular guy around. (Teachers are always talking about boosting the self-esteem of their students but I presume this is not an approved method.)

Playing Cards ~ 33

Mind you, this was the 50s so there were no sultry, come-hither super models, just semi-clad, almost middle-aged women with uni-brows wearing open kimonos or artfully draped bathrobes. Most of them looked as if they had peptic ulcers or would rather be someplace else. Didn't matter to us. We all thought they were just terrific.

That night all over Dhahran guys were rifling through top drawers and cigar boxes stashed way back on the top shelf of closets. The next day there were salacious playing cards all over the place and twice as many the day after that. Nudie playing cards had gone viral. Boys were trading them like baseball cards. "I'll give you this one of the red head in a girdle for that one of the blonde in the sailor hat with those short suspenders holding up her socks." Everything was fine as far as a certain demographic was concerned.

Wednesday morning Mr. Bricklin, the head of security, was spotted driving up to the school. Word spread fast. Cards were being shredded all over the place, toilets were flushed repeatedly. The bottom had dropped out of the nudie playing card market.

Eventually the usual suspects were rounded up and about six of us were sequestered in an empty classroom. Someone had fingered Cecil, so he was the first one called in for grilling by Bricklin. After what seemed like hours he came out and told the next kid to go in. Cecil was supposed to leave immediately and he did, but seconds later he returned to get his books and quickly whispered to a kid that he told Mr. Bricklin that he was walking down an alley, kicked a rock and found the card underneath. Word spread among us in about ten seconds. I don't know what the second kid told Bricklin, but the rest of us told him that while we had never seen such a thing, we had heard that a kid was walking down an alley, kicked a rock and found a card. Who knew that the alleys of Dhahran were paved in nudie playing cards? A stymied Bricklin finally left in a foul mood.

Looking back, it is hard to believe that the head of security of a major oil company would waste his time on some risqué playing cards. But you have to smile when you think that deep in Aramco's archives, somewhere between the drilling reports and the reams of seismographic records, there is an extensive investigative report on the case of the nudie playing cards.

The 10th Street Air-Conditioning Plant - 2001

THE GINGERBREAD BOY

Deceit is a many splendored thing. I didn't begin to master the subject until Smith and I, 16 years old and always hungry, were hanging around his kitchen. It was one of those windy days when shamaals swept the streets of Dhahran, the AC was quietly humming and there wasn't a soul outside except for some hapless Indian cook on the way back to his quarters after serving a bridge group luncheon, pedaling his bike in vain against the blowing sand

After we opened the refrigerator a half dozen times looking for something to eat, we wandered into the dining room to behold a giant gingerbread boy cooling on the typical Danish-modern dining room table. Smith picked it up and said, "My mom made it for my little brother's birthday. Do you want a bite?"

"Smith, no! Your mother would kill me."

"Oh well, she won't mind," he said, then bit the head off of Gingerbread Boy and gently laid the torso back on the baking pan. We wandered into his den to listen to Bo Diddly records and eventually drifted off to the Teen Canteen where we ate square hamburgers and burned decorative patterns into Dixie cups with cigarettes until someone or something turned up.

It didn't take long before we were joined by a half-dozen girls and guys, all of us waiting not for Godot but for something to do while the shamaal kept howling outside. Whether it was the Date Pit, the Surf Room or the Canteen, the drill was the same: Hang out and every time the door opened look up with expectations. The next person coming through just might open a world of possibilities.

And so it was that Dwayne walked in.

Dwayne was sort of special. His parents were divorced and he hadn't grown up in Dhahran but this summer his dad had brought him out for the summer. Definitely a fish out of water, he was fresh out of the sticks of Idaho, combed his hair in an elaborate sort of Brylcream-coated pompadour, didn't know from Saudi camp sandals with the tire treads, wore pearl-button cowboy shirts, had no clue that cut-off jeans were the ultimate in fashion and thought that Elvis was still the bomb.

When he first arrived in camp, a well-meaning but woefully misinformed friend of his father had asked Smith and me to help Dwayne ease into the scene. We thought it was a fairly hopeless project, but his single dad did have a fabulous bachelor pad on Christmas Tree Circle, an unlocked liquor cabinet, Playboy magazines strewn about and a killer Hi-Fi sound system. And, nobody was home in the afternoon.

It didn't take long to persuade Dwayne, and we were on our way to the apartment, picking up a few more desperately bored teenagers en route. Before you knew it, his dad's living room was packed with more than a dozen kids partying like mad. A bunch of us danced to the *Rolling Stones Now*, "Everybody needs somebody – to love..." while Smith rummaged through the cupboards looking for mixer. All of us were having a wild time – girls giggling, guys doing the monkey dance on the coffee table – when the front door came flying open.

Everyone froze. Dwayne's dad stepped in, hand in hand with some gal from the office, obviously intent on some kind of after-nooner. He looked at us. We looked at them. And then suddenly, as if in a cartoon, we vanished instantly out the back door leaving only a puff of dust and Dwayne in our wake.

Fortunately the famous Scott Miller lived directly across the alley and the party resumed at full throttle as we laughed and danced out the day completely oblivious to the wreckage we left behind.

A couple of days later I was at Smith's house. His mother was shooting darts of disdain at me. As insensitive and self-absorbed as I was at the time – a typical teenager – even I noticed her cold shoulder but didn't say anything. Years later, I asked Smith why his mom hated me so much. He finally admitted that she had asked him what happened to the poor gingerbread boy's head and he replied, "Tim ate it."

Guess that's what friends are for.

The Aramco DC-6 from New York arrives in Dhahran 1960s

FIRST STEPS

It's amazing how far the attitude towards smoking has changed in 50 years. In the 1950s I remember going with my mother to the doctor and after my exam the two of them smoking cigarettes while discussing my current affliction.

On those spectacular flights to New York and back on the Flying Camel or Flying Oryx, once the DC-6 was in the air, a great cocktail party would begin, especially on the departing flights. The cabin would be filled with people in the aisles, sitting on the armrests chattering away, drinking and smoking like it was a Christmas party in Dhahran.

Smoking on the plane was always a little close but perfectly acceptable. I once had a highly allergic friend who just resigned himself to being covered with hives by time he got to Shannon airport in Ireland. With the advent of the 707, the Aramco airline shut down and we all flew commercial. So it was about 1963 and Smith and I were flying on BOAC back to high school in the States when we witnessed an all-time first in air travel.

Once the plane was airborne the stewardess came on and announced that BOAC had just started a no smoking policy. If you objected to smoking you should switch seats now. And then she said, "For the duration of the flight smoking will only be allowed on the left side of the plane."

Smith and I laughed so hard that people started looking at us. "On the left side of the… (fill in your lame joke) became our tagline for the trip back to school. "Mustard gas is only permitted on the left side of the transit lounge." "Sauerkraut and Kielbasa sandwiches are restricted to the last three rows of the aircraft," etc. I guess even a child has to crawl before she walks, we were there for baby's first steps.

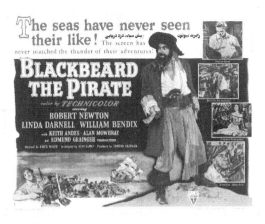

Finally a decent movie comes to camp

DHAHRAN'S PALACE OF DREAMS

Growing up in Dhahran in the 1950s without television and barely any radio, the movies were everything, our only link with the outside world. Three movies a week played with a fourth rerun on Thursday afternoon. As kids, we'd go to pretty much anything. Even if the feature was some unfathomable drama about thwarted love, boundless ambition or existential trauma in 1950s America, we'd go just for the pre-show features.

There would always be two cartoons, glorious big-screen, lovingly-made animated stories the likes of which today's children will never see: Mickey Mouse, Donald Duck, the incredibly violent Tom and Jerry or the nearly rabid Woody Woodpecker whose antics couldn't be shown these days without a R rating.

Once in a while Mr. Magoo or Droopy would wander across the screen as marvelously clueless as we were. In the later years we had the pleasure of watching the Road Runner duel Wile E. Coyote on the big screen.

For some strange masochistic reason, probably at the behest of those fine mothers who busily devised methods to get us out of the house, Aramco started a cartoon matinee once a week during our trimester vacations. It was sight to behold. Every Monday morning at 10, the theater would screen two hours of cartoons to a house full of kids. I'm fairly certain that most of the Recreation staff called in sick that day and those that didn't regretted it. The cartoons were gathered from a hundred features and spliced together by some patient Qatifi film editor. They also had cartoons that we had never seen before like Heckle and Jeckle, Mighty Mouse, Chilly Willy and even Crusader Rabbit.

There are 250 children twitching in the theater. The lights go off, and we are all swept into Looney Tunes: Bugs Bunny, Porky Pig, Elmer Fudd and the whole gang. The Tasmanian Devil makes a rare appearance. Then the film snaps. It's dark, quiet for ten seconds before the first stomping feet begin. Kids start chanting and soon everyone is stomping. The few remaining Recreation workers that couldn't get the day off decide to barricade themselves in the projection booth. Finally, the cartoons resume and we completely forget about the hiatus.

At the regular screenings, the newsreels were almost as fascinating as the cartoons. Somehow Aramco arranged to have an almost current supply of newsreels about the great, mostly incomprehensible events of the day – striking coal miners in the UK, various politicians in dozens of countries shaking hands one week and declaring war on each other the next. We had not the slightest idea what they were talking about but hurricanes, floods, earthquakes and train wrecks made an instant impression. Stories about the celebrities of the time – Marilyn Monroe, Elvis, James Dean – gave us the slightest glimpse of a distant culture that we sensed we should know better than we did.

As a young moviegoer, you were really out of luck if the pre-show trailers featured one of those travelogues by James Fitzpatrick, the only man who could make Mr. Rogers sound like Don Rickles on espresso. In each episode he would travel to some exotic location, shoot footage in a garish Technicolor that would make a Hawaiian post card look understated and then punish the audience with clichéd narrative and a voice that would make drying paint seem quick. It's too bad because he had some great footage but almost everyone in the audience couldn't wait until his signature sign-off, goodbye in the language of the country of the week: Adios, Au Revoir, Arrivederche, Aloha, etc., and not a moment too soon.

Then the feature would burst on to that beautiful, big screen and all of us, adults and kids, would step into a world so far away from Dhahran that you couldn't measure it. Most Hollywood hits were at least 8 months old by the time they made it to Aramco and that was considered current. Interspersed were films that nobody had ever heard of and nobody would again. Until the early 60s, most movies were in black and white, something that my own children can barely imagine. But the stories fed our starved imaginations like fresh bread.

Almost every opening night of every movie, no matter how obscure, was SRO for Dhahran's adults. For us kids at a matinee, the place wasn't crowded, it was air-conditioned, you'd get your dose of cartoons and if the movie bored you to death you could mess around with your friends in the first four rows.

There was a strategy to obtaining the choicest seats in the house in the middle of the front row. Clutching your crumpled riyal, you'd get to the theater early and wait at the head of the line. Then with ticket in hand you'd scramble for the far door and race down the aisle. At that age it was always a mystery to me why the teenagers would pass up prime seats in the front and cluster in the upper right of the theater at the back – no way to watch Daffy Duck. Anyway, we would assemble like sparrows on a telephone line across the first row and so on to the fourth or fifth. The show would start and so would the running commentary, "Did you see that! Wow, look, paratroopers over Malayasia. We saw that in Ceylon on our last local leave. Did you finish that paper for Mrs. Steinmetz? Quit jabbing me with your elbow. I don't like Gerald McBoing Boing cartoons. Amy just got her shipment, and tomorrow we can see her outfits. I'm sure that the Creature from the Black Lagoon could take down the Wolfman any day," and on and on. And if the movie mesmerized and spoke to us in any way, we became quiet and focused our senses on the 20-foot-tall images before us.

Of course not everyone was paying attention. The 10- to 12-year-old pre-adolescents were stuck between the front rows and the elite teenagers in the back. Voiceless, some of the young men affirmed their presence by a most ingenious device. In Khobar they sold cracker-balls, pea-sized paper fire crackers that you could throw to the ground and get a bang and a flash of sparks, five for a riyal.

By a miraculous process that I've marveled about before, a terrific invention – the coat-hanger slingshot – appeared out of thin air. By bending, usually in-artfully, a piece of coat-hanger then stringing a couple of rubber bands to a cloth pouch, any 11-year-old could have a perfectly serviceable cracker-ball delivery system.

Atlanta is burning. Scarlett and Rhett are yammering away and BANG! High on the left wall, a cracker ball explodes with a sharp snap and a great flash that illuminates the darkness. Now this is interesting. Vivian Leigh embraces Clark Gable, and three more cracker balls go off. The movie stops, the lights go up, the teenagers in the back are startled, and one of the guys from Recreation, probably Desai, strides down the aisle. At about the empty eighth row he finds three coat-hanger slingshots on the floor. In the tenth row a bunch of sub-teenagers grin back and the show goes on. After the movie all of us experience traumatic pupil dilation as we step into the bright, bright daylight.

Next to the swimming pool the theater was my favorite place, so I had many experiences there and beneath it. But the strangest event occurred on my way to the movies.

It was probably 1955 when some enlightened benefactor of the human race in Aramco Recreation decided that the theater needed a popcorn stand in front of the ticket office. We were excited. It was going to open on Wednesday afternoon.

Propitiously, that was also the opening of Blackbeard Meets Captain Blood or some similar low-budget pirate movie that promised action, cannons and sword fighting. I was so enthused that I went around with a rubber knife in my mouth for the week before, which didn't work out so well as the lead-based paint on the knife inflamed and infected the corners of my mouth. It probably infected my brain too as you will see. Nonetheless, a small price to pay.

Wednesday afternoon two friends came over and with our riyal and a half in hand we set out for Recreation one block away. What could possibly go wrong?

Being kids we couldn't just walk down the street, we had to use the alley and look for discarded treasures on the way. We didn't find any but we were charged up on dreams of popcorn and pirates. In the excitement, at the head of the alley about 10 feet from the cross street, I proposed a foot race across the street, past the playground to the popcorn machine. Great idea. Right there we assumed the stance. Ready, Set, Go! I raced out of the alley, into the street and straight into the path of a stake-bodied truck carrying a dozen gardeners. It was about 4 feet away from running me over when, in a sudden bolt of inspiration, I jumped as high as I could and went flying.

The next thing I knew I was sitting on the curb, about 20 feet away from the truck, my glasses askew, watching the visibly-shaken driver slowly walking up to me, contemplating his very short future. All the gardeners made themselves scarce. Before the driver got close to me, an Aramco sedan pulled up and a young American jumped out and came running over. With the truck driver hovering about nervously, he checked me out. There was no blood or broken bones, I could see two fingers and aside from being whiter than a freshly starched thobe, I was okay.

He very kindly drove me back to my house and walked me up to the door, opened it and then revealed that he was obviously a bachelor when he said, "You better go in and tell your mother."

I walked unsteadily down the hall to my parents' room to find my mother making the bed. She looked up and said, "Tim, why aren't you at the movies?"

"I got hit by a truck."

In my later years as a parent I've often wondered why she didn't just strangle me at birth. It would have been so much easier.

Dhahran - Dorothy Miller - 1961

THINK AHEAD

Think ahead. Be prepared. Always have a Plan B. These are the kind of concepts that my dad tried to pound into my head, and probably your parents did with you too. How hard could it be to remember them? The first two directives consist of only two words each. Pithy, sound advice, except that when you are 17, who needs advice?

You are way smarter than that because, though you don't know it, your frontal lobe isn't yet fully connected to the rest of your brain.

The frontal lobe comes up with marvelous ideas like wouldn't it be fun to ride a skateboard down a steep hill that crosses a busy intersection? Or my favorite that actually happened – wouldn't it be a kick to grab one of those deadly poisonous sea snakes at Half Moon Bay and handle it until it bit you? If this lobe was connected to the cerebral cortex the answers would be obvious but then the whole spontaneity thing would be lost.

My friend Smith and I were 17 and working in Sufaniya as apprentice divers for Al Gosaibi Diving Services. This was their first contract, and we worked from an old beat-up motorized dhow called *London*. Fanatic skin divers and spear fishers since the age of 12, we were in heaven.

The company was started by the legendary Dee McVay, a longtime IBBI/Bechtel diver in Arabia, and we were under the supervision of two contract divers from the states. Ed was a good natured, middle-aged, short, grizzly bear of a guy who had worked as a hard hat diver back East. "Yeah Tim, I used to make eight hundred bucks a day inspecting the sewer outlets of Baltimore harbor that spill into the bay. Black as night, literally walking through shit and toilet paper, 30 feet beneath the surface, couldn't see your hand in front of you. Payday I'd collect maybe three thousand or more – in cash. Monday morning I'd be back, broke as an old clock." The other diver was named Vern, lean and weathered, a bit mean, all he talked about was money. Of course, he would never have any because his second favorite topic of conversation was how he was going to hit it big in Vegas.

I do digress, but the point is that Smith and I were in Sufaniya on a Wednesday, *London* was being repaired so we were off until Saturday. There was a big party in Dhahran that night and another one in Abqaiq on Thursday. We had been paid, so we had almost three hundred riyals burning like fire in our cut-off jeans. In those days cab fare to Dhahran was something like a hundred riyals, so the obvious plan was to hitch-hike to Dhahran, clean up and party like it was 1964.

So after lunch in the middle of August – it couldn't have been more than 115 degrees – wearing cut-off blue jeans, Saudi Camp tire-tread sandals and white T-shirts with only cash in our pockets, we walk out the gate at Sufaniya and raise our thumbs.

Ten minutes later a big stake body truck with three guys in the cab, four kids and a half dozen goat-type kids in the back, pulls over. With a great exchange of Salaams, we are invited to hop on and we were on our way. Cruising down the blacktop at about 90 clicks, we have it made and are already making our plans for the night.

We drive about 20 minutes and the truck slows to a stop. What? The driver explains that he is now turning off to head straight to his tent somewhere deep in the desert. We watch him rumble off into the horizon and figure how hard could it be to get another ride. The novelty of hitch-hiking Americans was too much for any Saudi to resist. So we wait and sure enough, here comes a Toyota pick-up truck. Piece of cake. The driver slows up, and the guys in the cab wave as the truck keeps going. There are half a dozen Yemeni in the back with numerous bundles, not even room for a chicken.

No problem. We wait some more. Funny, it seems that there isn't much traffic at 1:30 on a Wednesday afternoon. Actually there is no traffic. After about half an hour we see a speck coming down the highway. It keeps coming until we can see that it's a bright blue Impala sedan. It slows down, we look alert and the driver gives us a big smile. He certainly would have picked us up except for the three other guys in the front and at least a half-dozen in the back. They all wave as the Chevy motors by. We listen to the drone of the engine grow fainter and notice that it's really hot. And silent. There's not even the hint of a breeze.

Smith: Jeez, I wish I had a hat.

Me: Yeah, that would be good.

Smith: I'm going to put my t-shirt on my head.

Me: Great idea.

So we put our t-shirts around our heads and wait and wait. Now it's well past 2 o'clock and still nothing.

Me: I'm tired of standing, I'm going to sit down.

Smith: Good idea.

Together: "Gadammit! It's hotter than hell," as we leap up.

Smith: Now I know why the Arabs always hunker down. Their sandals keep them from burning their butts.

We hunker. Minutes pass. Then more and more minutes.

Me: I saw a dead dhubb (large desert monitor lizard) a ways back on the road.

Smith: Probably Kentucky Fried about now.

Me: Yeah. I'm hungry. We should have had more for lunch than a Pepsi and French fries.

Smith: I'd kill for a glass of water.

Me: Water? Yeah that would be good. Hear that?

Way down the road we see a black splotch getting larger and larger. It's a giant Mercedes Benz water truck.

This is the ticket. It comes barreling along, getting closer until we can see the huge Somali driver and count them – four other guys in the cab. They all wave as they breeze past us.

Smith: Do you think Gayle will be at the party?

Me: Unless she's packing a chit from the ice house, do you think I care?

Smith: Ice? Now there's an idea.

Silence. We can hear the sun beating down on us. The heat is as thick as the humidity in Dammam. Time is slowing down. The idea of shade begins to grab our imagination. We look around. We are the highest object for miles in any direction. The blacktop begins to bubble.

Smith: You know some suntan lotion wouldn't be a bad idea.

Me: I'd kill you for a cold Pepsi.

Smith: I'd kill you and gut your uncle for a chilled Miranda.

Me: I don't like my uncle that much anyway.

Smith: I'd settle for tap water.

Me: Warm hose water would do me just fine.

Smith: At this point I'd drink the water at Imhoff Gardens. Here we go.

In the distance a battered white Land Rover comes rattling down the road. As it gets closer we can see that there is only a driver. Finally. We stand up and look bright. He drives closer and closer until he's about a hundred yards away and then hangs a right to go bouncing off into the desert.

Me: Damn it all!

Smith: Maybe we should follow him. Somewhere they've got some water.

Me: Damn it all.

Silence. It's getting onto 4 o'clock. Our tongues are rattling around in our dry mouths like twigs in a shoe box. We look up at the sun. It's still there. The blacktop bubbles some more.

Smith: I think my tongue is swelling up. Take a look, is it turning black?

Me: Let me look. Yeah it's not looking too good. You know if it really starts swelling up I'll have to lance it.

Smith: Lance it? With what?

Me: There's a piece of broken glass.

Smith: Damn! You stay away from me! If it comes to that I'll do it myself. Jeez.

Me: Okay, okay, okay! Just trying to be helpful.

Smith: What if it turns black?

Me: Well, no one's going to make out with you, that's for sure.

Smith goes silent as he contemplates the considerable implications of black tongue disease. A slight gust of wind comes out of somewhere and then disappears. One of those big black dung beetles crawls by. There's not a cloud in the sky. Time passes.

Smith: Do you hear something?

Through the heat waves rising off the asphalt, we can see a shimmering apparition tooling down the road. As it comes closer, we can see that it's big, it's red, it's a Dodge Fargo truck, it's Aramco. The driver pulls right up to us, rolls down the passenger window and says with a grin,

"You boys, waiting for the bus?"

We try to reply but our mouths are so dry it comes out as "Aauugha…."

"There's an Igloo at the back, have a drink."

"Thhhhaannx." We rush to the big, fat corrugated Igloo water jug strapped to the rear fender. It looks like a god. We start guzzling water, and for sure this guy has an ice chit. We drink about a half-gallon each and start feeling alive again. Smith has even forgotten about his black tongue.

We fall all over ourselves thanking him. The truck's idling and he's grinning. Inwardly he must be cracking up at the sight of our wild bug-eyes, sun-burned faces, shoulders redder than his truck, wearing t-shirts on our heads, but instead of laughing himself silly, he says, "Sure, you're welcome" and then puts the truck in gear… and pauses.

"I don't think the bus will be along for a while." Thinking to himself, like maybe never. "You guys like a ride?" Before we can answer, he says, "I'm Jim Ripley. Hop in," and boy do we hop. Thinking to ourselves, *How high, Sahib?*

We take off down the road. He says, "I don't usually put it on high but you'll like this." He leans over and turns the AC to mega-chill. Soon our core temperature returns to under a hundred. We know his oldest son David, an avid basketball player. Mr. Ripley goes into great detail how Abqaiq is going to destroy Dhahran in the upcoming Returning Students tournament in Abqaiq next weekend. We heartily agree.

He could have told us that Donny Osmond was the greatest rock and roll singer of all times and we would have agreed. We have a fine time. He drops us at the Main Gate and drives off. We didn't know it but Mr. Ripley was our Plan B.

That night the party is terrific. Gayle was there all right, with some college-age returning student wearing a Madras shirt and actual leather shoes – penny loafers with no socks that signal complete cluelessness. Smith meets up with a girl visiting from the tiny, isolated oil camp of Nariyah. After staring at the same three guys for months on end, Smith looks like Robert Redford to her and they have a great time. The next night we're off to the Friendly City for yet another wild episode in the town where it is never dark at night. We take a cab both ways.

Friday we're off to Khobar to look at switchblades and Zippos. In a rare instance of good judgment we buy baseball hats and sunglasses instead. That night another smaller but actually crazier party goes on past midnight. A few hours later at 4 in the morning, we hire a taxi to return to Sufaniya. We come dragging into the dining hall, and there's Ed chowing down on breakfast while Vern chain smokes Kools.

Ed puts his fork down and says, "Hi guys. How much money do you have left?"

"Twelve riyals."

"Good work. We'll make professional divers out of you yet."

Girl on her bike in Dhahran - Les Snyder 1947
The tennis courts are in the background

LOOKING FOR LANA

Since fourth grade at least, we all knew that we would be sent away after ninth grade to high school somewhere: Beirut, Rome, Switzerland, California or a military academy in Texas. By sixth grade it was an accepted fact of life. By eighth grade it was in our faces. Some kids welcomed it and others were uncertain about their fate, but we generally agreed that the kids whose parents couldn't bear to separate with their teen-age children and resigned to return to America were doomed.

Those kids would never experience the joys of being a returning student. We wondered about the parents too. I always figured that one of Aramco's deal-clenching recruiting pitches was that if you work for us, we'll guarantee that as soon as they are teen-agers we'll ship them out of the country for nine months a year.

Sometimes I wish I'd had that option with my own children when they became teenagers.

Now anyone in his right mind would do everything possible to avoid being in Arabia in the summer but we weren't even close to being rational at that age. Like almost every Aramco kid, I'd rather have ten root canals in a row than miss out on two weeks of the summer as a returning student. Many kids went to Rome or Beirut or Switzerland but I was brainwashed into going to the Benito Mussolini School for destroying social graces in the dying town of Prairie du Chien, Wisconsin –a Jesuit boys school on the edge of Hell. I must admit that there was a certain fascination to going to a school in America. I knew more about Rome and Beirut than I did the USA and thought that it might be interesting to sample the real American lifestyle – mistake number one.

So in 1962 I showed up on the banks of the Mississippi with a windbreaker and desert boots. No one told me that it'd be 10-below with 3 feet of fresh snow in a few months. Somehow I acquired a parka, sat on radiators all winter long and was finally released. For some odd reason I flew back by myself though my brother and a couple of friends went to the same correctional facility. I flew into the Rome airport and was wandering around waiting for the next flight when I bumped into the famous Jimmy R. who I had known since before Kindergarten. He was the kid who got caught by his foot upside down in the ficus tree by the swimming pool.

We were both travelling solo so we were as thick as thieves as we boarded the MEA, Middle East Airlines, flight to Beirut and then on to Dhahran. We landed in Beirut and then took off for the last leg when an engine burst into flames. We returned to Beirut. In those days, the airlines treated even 15-year-old teen-agers like human beings. They put us up in some hotel, not The Phoenicia, gave us meal vouchers and said they would pick us up in the morning.

It was traditional that parents would make sure that we had some cash on these trips, so between us we had more than a hundred bucks for "emergencies." That's like $500 today. It also happened that one of our classmates since third grade – who I should call "the most beautiful girl that ever walked the earth, Praise Allah" but will call Lana – had moved to Beirut in ninth grade when her dad was transferred to Tapline. So after dinner, Jimmy and I decided that we would find Lana. I mean, without an address or a phone number how hard could that be in a city of a million people?

We stepped out of the hotel into the taxi of Mr. Najib, a pot-bellied, older guy wearing a sweater-vest beneath a worn hounds-tooth jacket. Weary beyond his years, with the gentlest voice he asked where we wanted to go. We told him that we were looking for Lana and figured that ACS would be the logical choice. So off we went in his battered Mercedes, making our way through the chaotic traffic to the American Community School. Of course, when we arrived it was closed. Not only was it summer vacation but it was well past 9 o'clock at night.

Stymied, we wandered around in the front of the building for a while until Jimmy came up with a brilliant idea. "Mr. Najib, where do the American teen-agers hang out?"

Mr. Najib thought about it a minute and replied, "Kentucky Pizza," or something to that effect. So we headed to the Hamra and Kentucky Pizza. Mr. Najib pulled up to the front of the place, gleaming with bright purple neon, "Jailhouse Rock" blaring from within. We were certain that Lana would be here. We walked in to see three loud Lebanese teenagers drinking Cokes and smoking cigarettes. Behind the counter, the waiter and the cook were contemplating suicide. Well this wasn't the place, so we walked out to the sidewalk.

As we discussed our next option, Mr. Najib volunteered, "The Discotheque. Miss Lana must be there."

"Mr. Najib, you are a genius. Of course she would be there." And we set off for the Discotheque. Now, for those too young to remember, there were two Discotheque eras. The second one, Disco, was the Bee Gees, Donna Summer and Studio 54. The first one was twenty years before, mostly a European thing and consisted of lame French pop music and some by unknown English groups. Nonetheless it was all the rage.

Absolutely certain that we'd be dancing with Lana in mere minutes – of course we hadn't resolved the sticky question of who'd be dancing with Lana – we pulled up to a dark doorway somewhere in Greater Beirut. Mr. Najib said that he'd wait for us, and we went in.

Immediately we were confronted by a skinny, hatchet-faced guy who looked like a Beatnik all the way down to his scruffy Maynard G. Krebs goatee. We could hear music playing beyond a beaded curtain. Maynard took a look at us and tripled the price, "Ten dollars and a two-drink minimum."

"For both of us?" I said.

"No, no. One by one."

Well, the money was for emergencies and being absolutely ignorant we had no idea what "two-drink minimum" meant but behind that beaded curtain was Lana, so we pulled out the cash and were ushered in. It was a low-ceilinged room about 60 feet deep, 20 feet wide, illuminated by a single blue 40-watt bulb hanging somewhere halfway down the room. There were about a hundred guys and girls dancing in an undistinguishable mass of shadows.

A pretty young waitress in white boots came up and took us to a table the size of a medium pizza and asked, "What drinks you order?" This was completely new to us, so we said "Beer?"

She said, "No, only cock-a-tails."

This threw us for a loop as we had never drunk any cocktails. However we had heard our parents order drinks, so we exchanged a few words and said, "Tom Collins." And because we were so cool and understood the ways of the world and the two-drink minimum, we added, "Two each." She gave us the strangest look and walked off as Jimmy and I tried to adjust our vision to see what the hell was going on.

Gradually, as our vision adjusted to the dimness, we could see individual people dancing and the cloud of blue cigarette smoke piling up at the ceiling. The waitress came back, charged us ten bucks each and left us amid the French disco music and the gyrating Lebanese – none older than twenty-something.

We started on the drinks and they weren't too bad. About half way through we decided that even though we didn't smoke we should buy a pack of Winstons and another visit from Tom Collins. Fifteen bucks later we were smoking Winstons and drinking Tom Collins and generally living large. We got halfway through our third drink when Jimmy R. decided that we should seek out Lana. It was so loud and dark and smoky that we could barely discern between male and female but we set out for the back of the disco. No one even noticed us. They probably couldn't even see each other.

Eventually, we got to the back of the room and Lana wasn't there, which didn't bother us too much because we were starting to like lame French pop music and were generally getting loose with the Lebanese kids dancing in the smoky blue dimness.

On our way back to the table, a very pretty, petite Lebanese girl in the tightest skirt with long black hair and the biggest brown eyes was dancing apparently with herself. Jimmy, who was way more suave than I, started shuffling around, caught her eye and shortly they were dancing like Fred and Ginger. I was watching, just wondering how he does that so easily, when a big guy in a leather jacket, pegged pants and fence-climber shoes came out of nowhere and shoved Jimmy hard into some other dancers. This guy wasn't pleased but before he could follow up on Jimmy, some of the guys he had been pushed into started shouting at the big guy and someone shoved him back and I pulled Jimmy away.

We went back to the table, drained our drinks and made our way out of the disco to be met on the sidewalk by a concerned Mr. Najib who said, "Miss Lana? Did you see her?"

Glassy-eyed, Jimmy R. replied with a loopy grin, "No, but I danced with her sister," and then his legs turned to rubber and he settled to the sidewalk like a deflated balloon.

Mr. Najib drove us back to the hotel, and I gave him a twenty. Jimmy and I supported each other as we staggered into the lobby. The next morning the phone kept ringing and ringing until I realized it was for me and got up and answered it. The bus was leaving for the airport in ten minutes. I went into Jimmy R's room where the phone was still ringing and he was half dead on the floor. I woke him up, and we made it to the bus.

Our parents were at the airport in Dhahran. My mom came running up and said, "Oh Tim, how are you? We were so worried."

"Oh, we were fine. It was a little boring in the hotel, so we went out for pizza."

Ras Tanura - 1951

WALKING TO RAS TANURA

In 1964 on yet another misguided adventure, my great friend Ben Michaels, his older brother Roger and I decided it would be a great idea to walk to Ras Tanura. We ate a giant dinner at the Dining Hall and set off with one water bottle.

The first 10 miles are a breeze as we march through the desert into the dusk. There isn't much traffic, and the way to truly appreciate the desert is on foot. We watch the colors grow more intense as the sun falls into the horizon, what the Hollywood directors call the golden hour. It is a beautiful sight but when the sun finally sets it is extremely dark.

We hadn't thought to bring a flashlight, so we press on using a kind of foot braille to stay on the pavement. Fortunately a full moon emerges and we continue on in brilliant moon light. We might not have a flashlight but Roger does have a can of bright yellow spray paint. About 20 miles out of Dhahran we decide to graffiti the asphalt with cutting-edge social commentary.

A sophomore at the University of Oregon, Roger is naturally talented so he paints a giant duck and writes "Go Ducks!" Ben is a demented fan of the electric Blues guitar so he sprays out over a 10-foot stretch of highway "Bo Diddly is the King!" This might be considered as subversive in a monarchy but we figure no one has ever heard of Bo Diddly. Working vertically from the bottom to the top of one lane, I write four giant letters, L-A-N-A, so you can read it when approaching. Half way through the final A the can sputters empty so I can't paint the crossbar of the letter. It looks like an upside down V. In the morning hundreds of Qatifis will drive to Dhahran, see our clever handiwork and presume that Aramco has marked the pavement for some kind of road work.

Our water bottle vanished somewhere around mile 5, so 20 miles later it is getting a bit parched. We keep walking and eventually spot some kind of pump house in the distance. It is a small, well-lit installation about 100 feet off the road. We hurry up to the humming building certain that we can get a drink. No one is there. It's on automatic operation. This is Aramco, so there has to be a tap-water faucet here. No such luck. We plod back to the highway and continue on our way.

We are walking along about 3 in the morning when we see a shooting star. It keeps coming closer and closer before it turns into a bright, streaking trail of light that makes a loud crack when it hits somewhere in the desert not far from us, maybe a few miles away. It is spectacular.

Talking about the event for the next hours, with the consensus being that it was an alien spacecraft crash-landing in the desert, we make it to somewhere past Safwa where the road curves to Ras Tanura. Ben has a high-burn metabolism. He finally runs out of fuel, staggers off the road and keels over into the muddy roadside ditch of an alfalfa field. Covered in muck, he is sweaty, pale and his breathing is shallow. We drag him back to the side of the road. He smells bad too.

We wait in the humid darkness looking at the stars. Eventually a beat-up Chevy Impala taxi with three passengers pulls up, squeezes us in and drives us to RT. We were supposed to stay with Pam, Roger's girlfriend but arrive so early in the morning that we drink hose water and pass out like dead men in her front yard. On his way to work in the morning, Pam's dad sees us, especially Mike, still covered with mud and slime. Pam's dad is sure that we are random degenerates sleeping it off. He starts screaming at us. Of course, he has not the slightest clue that his daughter is running around with Roger.

Later on, Pam's dad's judgment of our character might have been more accurate when Smith, Ben and I went to Ras Tanura for the Tri-District dance. It was a very fun Tri-D as they always were and we separated into the night for various adventures.

About a half-hour before dawn I come limping towards the Surf House. I wasn't feeling quite as snappy as I was earlier in the night. At some point I had twisted my ankle while vaulting over a hedge for some already forgotten reason. Ben was sitting on the beach just back from the high-tide line staring blankly at the gorgeous turquoise water that's only found in Ras Tanura. Without saying a word I sit down next to him and stare straight ahead.

Not more than three minutes later Smith comes stumbling forth from under a porch somewhere. He looks like the real slow one in a zombie movie. Wordlessly, he sits on the other side of Ben, and we watch the blue-green chroma rise in the sea along with the dawn.

After a few minutes, backlit by the rising sun, a Russian wolfhound comes running down the surf line followed by a tall, beautiful young girl with blonde hair to her waist wearing a yellow bikini. She is gracefully skipping along like a gazelle on helium.

We don't move our heads. It takes too much effort. We just track her with our eyes from right to left until she leaves our field of vision. Once she is gone our eyeballs reset to straight on. No one speaks a word.

After a while, the sleek hound reappears along with the comely sprite running in the other direction. She disappears and we blink. It was really like the last scene in a Fellini movie.

We spend the entire bus ride back to Dhahran trying to figure out whether she was real or not.

Dhahran Swimming Pool. Steve Furman - 1939

THE SWIM MEET

As a child growing up in Dhahran I had an unrequited obsession with sugar – the more the better. At the time the Aramco commissary didn't have much beyond Droste chocolate, Black Jack chewing gum and O'Henry bars. Khobar had even less to offer: melted and re-melted, misshapen off-brand chocolate bars, hard candies and hopelessly expired soft candies from England such as the delicious Rowntree's Fruit Pastilles that were hard as pebbles by time they arrived on the shelf.

But being about 6 and ever vigilant, somehow I discovered that if you ate Jell-O concentrate you could ingest a whole bunch of sugar with the added thrill of some ungodly ingredients that made the whole concoction fizz in your mouth, sort of like the Pop Rocks that today's kids crave. So I started eating raw Jell-O. It didn't take long before my mother caught on, and the packs of Jell-O were placed far out of reach.

The cupboards in our kitchen were designed with about four or five levels. At the highest point there were a few narrow cupboards of no real use except they were out of easy access to everyone but Wilt the Stilt. That's where the Jell-O was stashed.

One day when everyone was gone I surveyed this dismal situation and then realized that by opening the cupboard doors and climbing the shelves as I went, I could scale up to the top cupboard and grab the treasure. So I pulled up the step-stool, hopped on the counter top and opening each door after another, I made my way to the top shelf like the Human Fly and snagged a bright, shiny package of grape Jell-O, probably the most toxic and desirable flavor of all.

I carefully climbed down, closing each cupboard door behind me. When I hit the floor I covered my tracks by moving the step-stool back into the pantry and escaped into the back yard where there were a couple of overgrown oleander trees. Within this thicket was a refuge I had discovered long ago and I proceeded to eat the whole package of grape Jell-O.

By the time Jell-O arrived in Saudi Arabia it was no longer a powder but rather a solid chunk of sugar and chemical additives. I sat there in perfect bliss breaking off piece after piece and enjoying every bite. When I was finished of course I wanted more so I licked the paper in perfect contentment with a blood sugar count of about point-30.

Finally, I sobered up enough to stand up and go back in the house.

I was greeted by my mom who said, "Timothy!" which was always a bad sign. "You've been eating Jell-O, haven't you?"

I was shocked. I had taken every precaution. How could she possibly know? I was oblivious to the fact that my mouth was ringed with vermillion and my tongue was dyed a deep purple. Oh well, one more night exiled to my room without dinner to contemplate what had gone wrong with a masterfully conceived plan.

With my fondness for sugar unabated it was inevitable that as time went on I would become a popsicle merchant at the swimming pool. The swimming pool was the center of Dhahran's recreational life.

As close as I can figure, the company built the original swimming pool somewhere around 1935. In a place where the temperature averaged 100-plus degrees in the summer, a swimming pool was a no brainer. The original planners didn't skimp on a crowd pleaser for kids and adults alike, and themselves, built a near-Olympic sized pool, the centerpiece of the early recreation complex. The north half was covered by a giant roof that covered the shallow end and hosted daily water volleyball games. The deep end was in the sunshine and capped with a diving board. In the late 40s there was even a high board elevated over the regular diving board.

Countless people enjoyed the pool. Around lunch time employees came and did their laps. Before and after, children swarmed the water like sea otters. Small kids played in the shallow end and the smallest cavorted in the baby pool under the watchful gaze of their mothers. In the deep end, the older kids lived or died on the diving board.

Anyone with grace and skill executed back flips, half gainers and swan dives off the board while the rest of us barbarians either dropped cannon balls or ambitiously attempted the Watermelon. This consisted of a cannon ball with one leg extended, the better to make a huge splash directed at the girls sitting on the edge of the pool. The left-hand side of the diving board was pretty much devoted to an unending game of Blindman's Bluff or Marco Polo.

In the mid-1950s the company had not yet opened the snack bar off the west side of the Teen Canteen portable, so there was a natural opportunity for the homemade popsicle vendor. Most every day there would be a couple of kids selling these tasty flavor pops at a half a riyal each. So naturally I plunged into this gold mine.

It was a fairly simple business. You would go to the commissary and buy some Kool-Aid, sugar, some 6-ounce waxed cups and a package of those small wooden Dixie cup spoons. Mix up the Kool-Aid, being careful to add about three times as much sugar as specified. Put the cups in the freezer, wait a bit to shove in the spoons and once frozen solid you were good to go.

There weren't any small coolers in those days, so you would store the popsicles in those larger wide-mouthed, 2-gallon thermos jugs and you were in business. A couple of kids arrived every day to sell their wares but I wasn't as driven so I maybe made it once or twice a week. Three or four of us would hang in the shade selling flavored ice – a perfect popsicle suq in the Saudi style.

It was all good until Patsy showed up. Not only was she a girl in the male-dominated popsicle trade but her thermos was decorated with ribbons and a hand-painted sign, "Patsy's Delicious Popsicles." And she smiled a lot.

To make it worse, Patsy had made her popsicles in layers of different Kool-Aid flavors, so she had a sort of rainbow popsicle – cherry, lime and grape. She was killing us with her marketing expertise Our only hope when Patsy arrived was that she would sell out, so we could unload our shoddy merchandise. This went on for a while until her dad was transferred to Ras Tanura and we could resume our tradition of sub-standard customer service.

Dhahran Swimming Pool - 1965

As time went on, I lost the entrepreneurial spirit. It cut into my time playing Blindman's Bluff, so I wasn't in business at the time of the biggest day at the swimming pool, the Tri-District Swim Meet.

This was a huge event with parents and kids from every district gathered around the pool.

There was every kind of conceivable competition: Inner tube races, swimming blindfolded, spoon races where you had to keep an egg in the spoon as you paddled the width of the pool, all announced in a dramatic play by play account over the PA system. Of course the biggest events were the Junior High contests in diving and swimming.

I was about 10 and I could swim twice the width of the pool underwater but was hopeless on the surface, so I wasn't in any races but just mingling in the crowd. I was lingering around the shaded west side of the pool when Mickey came running up. A chubby kid with a gap between his front teeth, Mickey's specialty was knowing everything that was going on and then broadcasting it to the world. We called him Scoop. He said, "Wow! It looks like Eddie Ronson has it locked."

Eddie was one of those guys who started shaving in seventh grade, a super athlete and a great swimmer among other things. Now he was a ninth-grader and for sure to win. For some reason, maybe because Mickey was such a know-it-all or maybe because I've always had a devil on my left shoulder, I said, "Well, I wouldn't be so sure. I heard that there is a kid from Abqaiq who swims like a porpoise. His name is Merwin Tish."

Who knows where I came up with the name Merwin Tish but it sounded about right. Mickey said, "Merwin Tish?"

"So I've heard," I replied, and Mickey was off into the crowd. As he rumbled off, I thought this is interesting, I wonder how far this can go?

So I wandered through the thronging crowd, occasionally mentioning Merwin Tish. By time I made it to the other side of the pool where the lounge chairs were splayed out in the sun, I saw Eddie's mother, Mrs. Ronson, lounging in a deck chair like Rita Hayworth. Somewhat younger than Mr. Ronson, she was someone I knew from before, the only Cub Scout den mother who wore nylons and high heels to the meetings. She said, "Oh Hi Tim. How have you been?"

"Fine, Mrs. Ronson. How are you doing?"

"I'm well, but I hear Eddie is going to have some real competition in the freestyle. Someone from Abqaiq."

Marveling at Mickey's efficiency, I said, "You don't say? I'm sure that Eddie will do just fine."

She replied, "Well I should hope so," as she flicked the ash from her Winston.

I wandered off, and of course Eddie smoked the freestyle race.

After the swim meet I was hanging around in the stream of people leaving the pool when a beleaguered Mr. Ronson, sun-burned and sweaty, came by burdened with towels, lounge chairs, a thermos jug and a gym bag. "Hi Mr. Ronson. How did Eddie do?"

"Well Tim, he won all right but it was close. It was a good thing that Tish kid didn't show up."

When Tequila was legal in Aramco
An AEA Dance at the Dhahran Patio -1950

TEQUILA!

Was just now listening to the radio when the song *"Tequila!"* by the Champs came on to carry me back to a much earlier time – 1957. The new Dhahran School had just been built on Third Street, and I lived on 11th Street which opened all kinds of opportunities for an unsupervised lifestyle coming and going. Maybe an hour of freedom each way. It was a proper school with a gym and a library, and I'm sure that there was a great education to be had there.

When the school first opened I started fourth grade. Our teacher introduced herself to this class of squirming 9-year-olds by saying. "Hello class, my name is Miss Hill. I want you to take out your paper and crayons. Okay, now I want you to draw the ugliest picture of me that you can imagine."

Wow! She threw down the challenge and I went right to work scribbling her hair as a bird nest and drawing big oval eyes, elephant ears and a long nose. I was lost in deep concentration putting scars on her cheeks when she came by and said, "Oh Tim, maybe you want to draw a big, nasty wart right on the end of my nose."

She got me with that remark and I was putty in her hands for the rest of the year. Miss Hill had a genius appreciation for the core principle of education – win their grubby little hearts and their minds will follow.

School was okay and all that but the best part was that Tommy M. lived on Third Street, directly across from the school. Sometimes Milt and I would loiter at Tommy's house after class. He was an excitable kid with an enviable brush-cut that stood straight up about 3 inches high. Enthusiastic about life, Tommy was the only kid in camp who had a mini-motorbike and, better yet, his parents weren't home during the day.

We'd hang around his room and discuss the world seen through the eyes of a 9 year old. We talked about the latest war movie, the dead jackal we saw on the road to Khobar, the kids at school and gross teachers but mainly we discussed the proven fact that girls were from another galaxy. Completely mystifying. You wanted so much to amaze them and hear their laughter but they were working from an entirely different script.

Take for instance one of those big green hedge worms that apparently thrived on Aramco's DDT as much as they did on the company's hedges. Show that caterpillar to Lana and she'd go "Yuk!" and get mad at you. Show it to

Milt and he'd be delighted and say, "Boy, that's wicked. Let me see it! Can I squash it?" How could anyone think that those caterpillars weren't fascinating?

Sometimes their undulating bodies with all those feet working in unison as they crawled up your finger, their gesticulating antenna searching for a signal would mesmerize us and we'd put them unharmed back on the hedge. We probably understood them better than we did the opposite sex. It was just that we couldn't stop talking about certain girls.

Tommy had an older brother who never seemed to be around. He always had the latest 45 records, so one day Tommy comes up to me just before the end of class and says, "You've got to hear this."

"What?"

"You've got to hear it," he said and then dashed off.

Minutes later, Milt and I breathlessly knock on Tommy's door. He opens it with a giant grin, "Gentlemen, right this way."

The air conditioning is humming throughout the house. The shades are drawn as we silently walk past the classic Aramco thick-bodied maple furniture in the living room, past the Danish Modern dining table and follow Tommy into his room. He goes over to the dresser and intently drops the needle on the record player.

And there it was for the first time in Saudi Arabia!

A hand clapping rhythm, a guitar, a building Latin beat, a blasting saxophone that couldn't be resisted and then, "Tequila!" After the first riff, we are all up moving around in some unidentifiable dance.

Laughing and gyrating, getting ready to shout "Tequila!" at the right time. We have no idea what Tequila is but it sure sounds like a good idea.

We must have played that song dozens of times before the Champs had us sweaty and worn out. Walking home through the deserted alleys of Dhahran that evening I finally realized that girls might not be so mysterious after all. It sure would have been fun to rave on to *"Tequila!"* with Lana.

Colonel Stapp's Famous Rocket Sled Ride - 1955

HIGHER LEARNING

We've all gone to school for endless years but it's rare to remember a certain day when you actually learned two separate things.

In 1952 I went to Dhahran Kindergarten in the portable, pre-fab building that later became the infamous Teen Canteen. In first grade I went to the portable close by that eventually became the Hobby Shop. What a great place. Anyone could come in and use all this marvelous equipment: drill presses, table saws, grinders, belt sanders and the like. Much later in life, my friends and I scrounged up pieces of flat metal and made a variety of swords and edged weapons that enabled us to swack and hack at hedges and oleander branches all over camp.

I only remember a couple of incidents from first grade. Right away I tried to duplicate my hooky playing exploits from Kindergarten but they were on to me and I only managed a pitiful two days. The second thing I remember was that it was around Thanksgiving and we had to color in various pictures of Pilgrims and Indians, turkeys and cornucopias. I had an Indian picture that I enthusiastically put the old crayons to.

When the day was over, we all had to line up at the door. The teacher came down the line looking at our great artwork. She stopped at me. She took my Indian chief and held it up to say, "Children. This is not the way to color a picture. Tim has colored outside the lines."

I was stunned. This was my masterpiece. How could she not see how brilliant it was? Oh well, there are none so blind as those who will not see. I imagine the teacher thought that she was giving me a lesson in life but it backfired. I distinctly remember thinking to myself, "If that's the way you want to play it, I'll never color inside the lines as long as I live." And that pretty much determined my destiny for years to come.

In second grade I finally went to school in the actual school building, the original one that later became half-pool hall and half-library. Our classroom had about twenty kids and it felt like a real place of higher learning.

At the time one of my good friends was Ralph W. He was big for his age, very shy, and really smart with an avid interest in science and technology. We were both enamored with aircraft and rockets, so one day at the movies we were electrified by the newsreel that showed Air Force Colonel Dr. John Paul Stapp nearly breaking the sound barrier on a rocket sled.

Strapped into that contraption, when the rocket was ignited, he went skating down the rails at 623 miles per hour, faster than a 45-caliber bullet. What blew us away was the footage of his face being distorted by the massive G-forces. At the end, when the sled braked in 1.4 seconds, Colonel Stapp was subjected to 43 G, the impact of hitting a brick wall at 120 miles an hour. His cheeks were bulging like water balloons, his eyeballs popping out of their sockets, his jaw distended. We were amazed.

We had a new hero for our pantheon and, though the movie was entirely forgettable, we arranged to meet up the next day to go to the film just to see the newsreel again.

For some reason I was seated in the front of our classroom – probably so the teacher could keep an eye on me. Ralph sat right behind me. The teacher was demonstrating cursive writing on the black board, so I turned around to make some smart-ass remark to Ralph. Before I could say a word, right before my eyes one of the long fluorescent lamps on the ceiling gave way on one end and the whole fixture came swinging down like a pendulum to nail Ralph right in the side of the head. He just vanished from his seat as the dangling fixture sparked and smoked above his desk.

Pandemonium broke out. Bleeding from his head, Ralph was unconscious on the floor and we were all screaming and yelling. Finally order was restored, and we were sent out of the classroom. The ambulance came for Ralph who by this time was barely conscious and severely cross-eyed.

Milling around outside after Ralph was hauled away, I happened to meet an administrator named Louis, an articulate, lean, handsome Palestinian who worked in the principal's office. He hadn't heard the news so I immediately told him about Ralph's accident. When I finished, he asked me if Ralph was injured. I had never heard the word "injured" before, so I asked him what that meant. He explained that it meant "was he hurt?" Yes, he was hurt all right; he was hammered right out of his chair by that light fixture.

So on that day in second grade I learned two things. The meaning of the word "injured" and, more importantly, just when you least expect it, some damn thing will come out of nowhere to hit you upside the head. It was a defining moment in my education.

Actually, it was probably the most important lesson that I ever learned in my life.

Ralph showed up at school a few days later with a massive bandage wrapped around his head. After sixth grade, his dad left the company and I never saw him again.

Colonel Stapp survived the rocket sled ride with fractured ribs, two broken arms and permanent retinal damage that left him partially blind in one eye. That didn't deter him. and he went on to ride the sled countless times as he devised safer seats and restraints for Air Force pilots. He was the inventor of the crash-test dummy and became a huge champion of seat belts in cars, thereby saving tens of thousands of lives.

Fittingly, as in the case of Ralph, when a Major Murphy rigged all the electronic sensors on Stapp's rocket sled backwards - so that all the instrument readings were zero, Stapp coined the famous theorem known as Murphy's Law: "If anything can go wrong, it will."

Later he composed Stapp's Law: "The universal aptitude for ineptitude makes any human accomplishment a miracle."

Stapp had vowed not to marry until he finished his dangerous work with the rocket sled, so he was 48 when he married Lillian Lanese, a ballerina with the famous Ballet de Russe de Monte Carlo. Eight years later he was present when Lyndon Johnson signed the Mandatory Seat Belt Act. In 1999 our hero Colonel Dr. John Paul Stapp died at the age of 89 in Alamogordo, New Mexico.

And I've always wondered where Ralph is these days.

The Dining Hall - 1962. Courtesy of Yousef Al Khan

THE SECRET DOOR

With the end of World War II, Aramco was finally able to ramp up production and start making some money after sinking tens of millions of dollars into the Arabian venture since 1933. While building housing like mad, in late 1947 the company started to build the large community projects. The first big complex was the Dining Hall which incorporated the actual dining hall plus the bakery, the butcher shop, commissary services and all the various departments that would support the feeding of the employees in all three districts.

Aramco was known for utilitarian architecture but when they designed the Dining Hall the architects went the extra riyal, actually many riyals, and incorporated the giant cubic façade for the facility that wasn't really absolutely necessary. It was likely at the direction of then current president James MacPherson who had a flair for the big gesture. The Dining Hall's entrance added 20 feet of cement block faced with cut limestone that gave the facility a special grandeur that is now iconic.

Nowadays the company would have found a sponsor and called it something like the Kaki Kola Convention Center, but being Aramco they settled for a giant DH logotype with the words Dining Hall. Since the facility handled the daily feeding of hundreds of employees as well as serving as the reception hall for countless dignitaries, it was strategically located at the intersection of the entrance road from the main gate and King's Road.

The Dining Hall was the nexus of Dhahran. Meanwhile that giant cube over the entrance was always present, and who could pass the Dining Hall without wondering what was contained inside that enormous volume.

It was 1962. I was a sophomore in high school and returning student, the lowest level of the social pecking order. I was coming back from an excellent shop class that the company offered returning students to teach them how to design simple projects and use power tools like a table saw without cutting your thumb off. Meandering back from Aramco's shop area as I approached King's Road, I noticed that the company had torn out the vegetation along the western annex of the Dining Hall and replaced it with a trellis and new plants.

It looked as if someone could climb up the trellis and get to the roof. I stopped and looked a little harder and noticed that there was a small door leading directly into the stone-clad cube over the entrance. I wondered where the door might lead to and then walked on.

A couple of nights later I was hanging in the Teen Canteen with Smith and a couple of girls. It was a quiet night. Mohammed Hampton who ran the Canteen was cleaning up for the day. The jukebox was out of order, and I suspect that Mohammed had something to do with the outage.

He had worked for the Hamptons for many years, so in addition to his wonderful personality he had an innate understanding of how to deal with American teenagers. No one knows how many hapless Saudis had fled in horror from this particular demographic, but Mohammed had the right stuff, with one exception. Though he could listen to wild Bozuki music all day long, Rock and Roll sent him up a tree.

So we sat there drinking Pepsi and waiting for the next thing, a peculiar canteen ritual wherein you would hang there and wait for the door to open. Someone would appear and they were either someone you wanted to see or someone else. The feeling was mutual and often the door opener would flee back into the night. No one opened the door that night, so we talked with Jenny and her friend Marie who hardly ever said a thing, unlike Jenny. She had grown up next door to Smith, their parents were close friends and she was a year younger than Smith. She was gorgeous in most every way but her goal in life seemed to be to make his life miserable – she was like Smith's little sister. She was showing us her latest purchase from a shop in Khobar.

"I just got this today," she said waving her ring to us. "It's pure gold, with this beautiful inset."

Smith said, "It's not pure gold. How much did you pay for it?"

"He wanted thirty riyals. But I got it for ten."

"Let me see it," said Smith.

"Here look at it," as she put his finger out for him to look.

"No way it's pure gold."

"Well, maybe it's gold plated. But it's set with a scarab."

"A scarab?"

"Yes, it's a scarab beetle carved out of a semi-precious green stone. It is very lucky."

"Semi-precious means it's not precious. Lucky? It would have been luckier if you hadn't bought it."

"Smith, what do you know about lucky? You're lucky that you weren't smothered at birth."

"Jenny."

"Oh okay, that's a little harsh. You're lucky that I even talk to you."

Marie giggled. I was rolling my eyes wondering if this banter would ever end, so I said, "Nothing is ever going to happen here tonight but I found a secret door."

"Secret door?" said Jenny.

So I told them about this small door over the Dining Hall, and they agreed that we should go check this out rather than grow old hanging around the canteen. So we set out.

It was one of those nights that is so humid the water vapor forms halos around the street lights. As we travel down King's Road we meet two girls who are wandering around Dhahran in search of something to do. After a brief meeting they agree that the secret door is definitely worth pursuing and we continue on.

Aerial view of the Dining Hall complex

Of course I have no idea what is behind the secret door but I am committed now, so we press on. As we approach the Dining Hall we all go into stealth mode and scurry across the street, past the circular brick bench that contains the giant ficus tree in front of the entrance. We press ourselves against the wall of the building as if the searchlights of some maximum security prison are constantly searching for our presence. It is ten o'clock on a Monday night, not another soul in sight.

    We slink over to the trellis. Sure enough, it had been built out of welded pipe to Aramco's industrial-grade specifications. A hippopotamus could scale it without a problem. I climb up the trellis and before you know it Smith, Jenny, Marie, the two girls and I are on the roof of the Dining Hall. We make our way over to the secret door and to my relief it is actually there. About 3 feet tall, the wooden door looks as if it's never been opened. I turn the latch and tug at the door but it's been painted over so many times it doesn't budge. Smith, who is larger than me by forty pounds, gives it a try and finally it swings open.

I peer into a dark void. It looks as if there is a landing a few feet down, so I crawl down and after a minute or so I find a light switch, and a dim overhead light now illuminates the whole space. It's like a huge cavern.

There is a catwalk suspended from the roof and all around are vertical guy wires holding up the ducting and the false ceiling. The catwalk extends about 30 feet to an opening on the opposite wall. How could we resist? I start across the catwalk, followed by Smith, Jenny, Marie and the two girls.

The lint and the dust from hundreds of shamaals curl up in faint clouds with every step, and the vertical supports of the catwalk start to ping with tension. It occurs to me that maybe the catwalk isn't designed to hold six people walking close together, so I ask everyone to spread out.

We walk on, fascinated by all the guy wires hanging down to support the ceiling. What seems like hundreds of wires, undisturbed for ages, glisten in the weak light. With each step there is a groaning from the catwalk, occasionally there is a sharp noise, but we make it to the other side of the cavernous cube.

There is an opening, and we pass through to a shallower, much wider void with what seems to be thousands of vertical wires holding up a great expanse of false ceiling and AC ducts. We start walking over the expanse of the actual cafeteria headed for the opening on the other side. Jenny stumbles and Smith grabs her before she goes falling head-first through the false ceiling into the dining room. Marie giggles and Jenny is irate, "I wasn't going to fall. Hands off of me." Smith realizes that whatever he does, he is doomed.

I pass through the opening to a ladder that goes below. I scramble down, the others follow and we are in the kitchen of the dining hall. It's brightly lit and all buttoned up for the night –everything is put away, the counters are all cleaned up – ship shape. However, being teenagers who are always hungry, we immediately look for something to eat. The refrigerators are locked and there aren't any pantries we can get into, so we start poking around.

Finally Jenny says, "Aha, ice cream!" The glass-topped, horizontal deep freezes that hold the ice cream aren't locked. There are 5-gallon containers of vanilla, chocolate, strawberry, coffee and hazelnut ice cream staring right at us. We look around the kitchen and Smith says, "There aren't any spoons!"

Jenny replies, "Who needs spoons?" and plunges her hand into the strawberry and pulls out a fistful of ice cream and proffers it to Smith. A feeding frenzy ensues, though nobody wants any coffee or hazelnut.

We are all having a great time gorging on fistfuls of ice cream when Marie pipes up to say, "What if we get caught?"

Caught! For what? We were merely walking across the roof of the dining hall, found an open door and strolled into a maze that ended up in the kitchen. It wasn't our fault that we were famished after all that effort.

Nonetheless, even though we are absolutely blameless of any wrong doing, we know that we had better leave.

Being smarter than the rest of us, Jenny takes a wet paper towel and smoothes over our claw marks in the ice cream. We make our way up the ladder, across the expanse of the cafeteria ceiling, through the opening, back across the great cavern of the entrance and out the secret door onto the roof. Carefully we descend the trellis and step out on the lawn. A taxi cab passes but the driver could care less, and the night is as still as when we entered. We gather at the giant ficus when Jenny says, "Damn it Smith. I lost the scarab on my ring." As if it was his fault.

He says, "I guess it wasn't as lucky as you thought."

She says, "You're lucky that I even knew your name and I think I just forgot it," and marches off with Marie. The two other girls have had a great time for a Monday night and drift away. Smith and I discuss the evening's events, and he heads off for Sixth Street while I walk down King's Road to my house.

About half-way down the length of the dining hall complex I start laughing.

I can just see some grizzled geologist making his way over from Exploration for lunch at the Dining Hall – a hot, open-faced turkey sandwich with mashed potatoes, followed by a cup of coffee and a bowl of strawberry ice cream. And on the second bite, how lucky he will be to not crack a molar on a scarab beetle.

With Bea and Theo - 2012

KANGAROO BIKES

A couple of weeks ago I first saw this photograph of me standing with my two grandchildren. Bea is 6 and Theo is 3. They are lively, bright, funny, and unlike most of society, actually enjoy my company. They are positive proof of the wise old adage, "If I knew how much my fun my grandkids would be, I would have had them first."

However, looking at this picture and their smiling faces, what struck me the most is just how damn short they are. When you are at their age your life is measured in how far you can reach. The first time you climbed the back-door steps alone, your first doorknob – in a year or two you will be able to hit the light switch.

When Bea was three there was a big Christmas party at my daughter's house. Presents stacked up in the corner under the twinkling tree, the dining table decked in holly and poinsettias covered with little presents, funny Christmas cards, tasty appetizers and a big plate of colorful Christmas cookies.

A half-hour into the party music was playing, more than two dozen guests were milling around the living room talking and laughing and, most critically, paying no attention to Bea in the dining room. I was watching her circle the dining table out of the corner of my eye.

She was tall enough to see that there were cookies on the middle of the table but sadly not tall enough to snag a few. She considered this problem for about twenty blinks and then quickly dragged one of the dining chairs up to the table, hopped up, snatched three cookies and then leaped down in one fluid motion like a mongoose that had just stolen a cobra egg.

I was deeply impressed by her technique, but Bea won my heart when she pushed the chair back against the wall before she scampered off to her room to gorge on Frosty's head or Santa's icing-covered thigh. Without my expert coaching, she knew by instinct to cover her tracks.

Being short has its challenges. I guess that's why growing up I was always looking for an edge and when I was about eight I found one. My buddy Milt had a curious, inventive mind. Once in fourth grade we were all assigned a take-home science experiment to blow flour out of a straw across a candle. It would make a huge flame thus demonstrating the volatility of fine particles of most anything.

When Milt went home to try this he couldn't find any straws, so he rolled up a paper tube about the size of a cigar, packed it with flour and blew it across the flame. Actually he blew out the candle and spewed a huge blaze of flour across the kitchen. Undaunted, he tried it again only to blast another flour trail across the floor.

This wasn't working out until Milt was inspired. He got a paper bag and placed it on the other side of the candle to catch the flour when it blew by. He rolled another flour cigar and puffed with all his might. The flour ignited into a giant fireball that shot into the paper bag and rebounded straight into his face. The next day Milt came to school with rosy red cheeks, no eyelashes and his eyebrows mere stubs.

One day Milt and I saw a picture in Life magazine of some kids walking on stilts and decided to build a couple pairs. My dad had a shed with tools and a wood pile, so Milt came over and we sawed off a couple of two-by-fours and nailed on some short blocks for foot-holds. We wanted to test the first pair but decided that we had a death-pact to build both sets and then try them at the same time. Sweating and huffing, we finally finished and, dying of excitement, simultaneously hopped on our stilts. Elated for about two nanoseconds, we collapsed into each other like spastic praying mantises and crashed to the lawn. Milt said, "Boy, that was cool!" I laughed and we were back up on our new legs.

After a while we could walk two steps before keeling over, then three, and so on until we could walk for hours on those sticks. We used to go up and down the sidewalks of Eleventh Street from the Hamilton House back to Recreation, off the curb onto the street, back on the curb, clip-clopping past those lovely cut-limestone walls that we were now tall enough to see over.

We always hoped that we'd see something exciting, maybe a robbery being committed, a body being buried or at least Lisa Swenson sunbathing in the back yard, but all we saw was a gardener trimming the hedge or an overweight Mr. Swenson in his undershirt chewing a cigar while contemplating some deep truth as he watered his front lawn in the dusk. Nonetheless, what we actually saw wasn't as important as the fact that we were now 2 feet taller and might be able to see wonderful things. Expert stilt-walkers, we had a great time walking all over camp. Once we even made it from the swimming pool to the Mail Center without falling off once.

So time goes on and we're taller but still can't jump high enough to reach the top of the door jamb. I'm over at my friend Will's house. Will was a terrific guy. Alert, light-hearted, both smart and clever. Later on in eighth grade he could open any Master combination lock in the locker room purely by touch.

We are in his back yard playing with a Rocket Sled that his dad Gus helped him build. It's the coolest thing, a 6-inch piece of broom stick painted yellow with a deep hole drilled into one end and an eye hook screwed into the top of each end. The eye hooks are threaded by a clothes line stretched across the back yard to form a hanging broom-stick monorail.

Will pulls out one of those small CO_2 cylinders used for seltzer bottles and shoves it into the hollowed-out hole at the back end of the broom handle. He pulls the sled back to the end of the clothesline and then, tightly holding the sled and a ten penny nail centered on the head of the gas cartridge in one hand, he hits the nail with a hammer. BLAM! The rocket sled travels the back yard at sub-sonic speed. This was too good to be true, and we go through half a dozen CO_2 bottles before Gus comes in the back gate from work.

"Hey guys, how are you doing?"

I say, "Oh fine Mr. Meadows. The Rocket Sled is the greatest thing."

"You think so? How's it working?" He starts checking out the rig. "Will, maybe if you re-tie that end to the hibiscus and make it even tighter we can get a longer run." As Will does, that, Gus puts another bottle into the sled and picks up the nail and hammer.

"Hey, Will! Are we ready?" Will gives the nod and in one smooth move Mr. Meadows launches that sled down the line. It blisters past as a blur and crashes into the hibiscus. Our jaws drop. Thor walks among us.

"That was a pretty good run. William, guess what I saw coming home tonight? A Kangaroo bike!"

"A what?" We both say.

"Yeah, some kid was riding a Kangaroo bike."

"What's that?"

"We used to make them when I was a kid." Going over to Will's bike Gus shows us. "You take the pedals and sprocket assembly from an old bike and weld it into the frame right in front of the seat. Then you run a longer chain back to the rear wheel. Put a long pipe on the seat and handle bars and you're sitting on top of the world."

Already our brains are spinning trying to figure out where we could scrounge a derelict bike.

Then, because Gus Meadows is a mechanical engineer who loves kids and backyard projects, he says, "I'll tell you what. You and Tim get some old bikes, Thursday I'll get out the welder and we'll make two Kangaroo bikes." I was walking on sunshine.

Dhahran was a very small town. When something new appeared it was a sensation. I don't know who the first kid was to ride a Kangaroo bike but he set off a frenzy. Gus made each of us wear welding goggles when he welded up our bikes. He showed us how to take two chains and make them into one long custom-sized chain, how to adjust the handle bars and set the seat. When we wobbled off down King's Road on our brand-new bikes we were the kings of the asphalt. Quickly a Kangaroo bike subculture emerged: Almost a dozen 10 or 11-year-olds cruising around Dhahran, a couple feet above the hoi polloi and many degrees cooler than the average person.

The thing about Kangaroo bikes is that they are difficult to mount. It's best if you have a high curb to start from. Otherwise you have to make a sort of flying leap up to the pedals and hope that you can control the bike before you lose balance and crash to the street. So when you're up, like a shark you keep moving.

Dhahran - 1958

I'm fairly sure that my life peaked at 11 when I had my Kangaroo bike. I was 7 feet tall and as suave as I'd ever be in white socks, my jeans rolled into a cuff, my short sleeves too. At the time I lived by Wildroot hair tonic. I'd rub that industrial-grade lanolin into my head, brush my hair straight back, and then, from left to right, I'd run the comb over my head to create the latest up-to-the-minute hair-do. Only Satan knows why I thought that was a good look.

One time my very proper Aunt Mary visited, and after cleaning up from a day at Half Moon Bay I came walking out with my pompadour in place. She looked at me and said, "Tim, what have you done to your hair!" as if I had come out in dreadlocks with my face tattooed. Anyway, I thought I was on the cutting edge and to prove it I was wearing quasi-Buddy Holly glasses before I knew who he was.

It was a humid August night at the top of Eighth Street, the street lights have just flickered on and the asphalt is still radiating heat as five riders approach. The Kangaroo riders from Hell are gliding down the street like a pod of dolphins, laughing and shouting all the way. Nobody can stop the Kangaroos.

Milt is especially wired, cutting back and forth between us, hollering and pedaling like mad, lifting his butt up to pretend that he is passing wind. Sophisticates one and all, he's so funny that we practically fall off our bikes and then pretend that we are falling off our bikes. Cruising past the houses and the six-unit apartments we approach the intersection of Eighth and Hoover Street which runs straight down from recreation.

In a good example of a corporate brain-burp, Aramco had started a program of embedding giant metal traffic-buttons at street intersections in the heavy equipment yard. From there someone had decided to try this technique in the residential area with the result that there was one lone steel button about 3 inches high and as wide as a medium pizza embedded in the middle of the road on the east side of Hoover and Eighth.

One day, wearing his traditional white shirt, District Manager Ned Scardino was driving down Hoover Street when he hit that safety-button with a cup of coffee in his hand. The program was abandoned, though the button remained.

As we approach the cross street, Milt zooms ahead of us and says, "Let's go to my house," and then swings a wide arc east onto Hoover. We follow in a tight formation like the Blue Angels at some air show. Milt looks back at us over his shoulder and says, "This is the best," just as he hits the giant traffic-button and, with the most amazed look on his face, goes hurling over his handlebars to land head first onto the asphalt.

"What was that?"

Somewhat concerned, we approach Milt's lifeless form sprawled out under the streetlight. The only thing is that we are on Kangaroo bikes so we can't stop pedaling or we'll fall over. Milt seems to be alive but he doesn't seem to be breathing.

He starts moaning, so we keep circling around him. After a while he clutches his hand and twitches his leg. He isn't paralyzed. We ride easier. All of a sudden, Milt jumps up bleeding from ear to chin. He pulls up his t-shirt to wipe the blood off his face and says, "That was wicked. This will make the greatest story someday."

We yell our approval. Overjoyed that we didn't have to dismount to call an ambulance, we ride in loops until Milt can limp to the curb and jump on his bike. We form up and head off towards Sixth Street. Once again the Kangaroo riders are on the loose and Dhahran is at our mercy.

A Middle-aged Bedouin - 1939

ABU HAMID

It was November 18, 1978. Two years earlier I had started a video electronics business in Jeddah that serviced video equipment, installed closed circuit TV systems in hotels, hospitals and compounds and distributed the only legal video programming in a country awash in bootleg videos.

I lived with my wife Janet and two children, Khamisah and Luke, in the bottom flat of a villa owned by Shaikh Salman, a local *Qadhi*, an Islamic judge. A very cheerful fifty-something Hijazi, he lived above us with his wife and four young daughters. His villa was located in what was in those days referred to as Somali town, a neighborhood halfway between the main North-South boulevard and the coast road.

Like every other residence on the street it was surrounded by a 10-foot wall, so when I stepped out the front gate that morning at 5 o'clock there was nothing but a dark, empty road, blank cinder-block walls on both sides and the vaporous humidity that hung like fog.

I was waiting for a taxi to take me to the airport for an early flight to Riyadh. And then I waited some more. Finally in the distance I saw a tell-tale yellow Datsun cab coming my way. Apparently it had some alignment problem as it looked like a crab. The front wheels were about a foot to the left of the rear wheels but it came rolling on. As it got closer, I could see that the left headlight was never going to shine again and the fender had been modified with a ball-peen hammer.

I heard the radio blaring as the cab approached, and as it slowed almost to a halt I was able to see the driver. An ancient, wrinkled Bedouin with a long gray beard, he looked like the grandfather of some Biblical patriarch. He eyed me with nothing but suspicion, decided that I was some sort of demon from the inner reaches of hell and speeded up. About 50 feet later he stopped. Even demons could be a paying customer.

I walked over to the cab and put my head in the window. Giving me a tight-lipped stare, he barely nodded, begrudgingly he'd let me ride in his cab to the airport. I got in the back and he started up. The shift between first and second gear was a little noisy, the transmission needed some work but otherwise we drove along quietly for about a minute until he pulled to the side, turned down the highly-caffeinated newscaster on the radio and shut off the engine. I thought to myself, *Here it comes. Some kind of rant about me being a foreigner ... or worse.*

The old man took a second to compose himself and then slowly turned around, glared at me through rheumy eyes and said in angry Arabic. "Jimmee Jones! What in the hell is this Jimmee Jones?"

I took me a few seconds to figure out what he was saying because Jimmy Jones was the last name I ever expected to hear at five in the morning in a dark street in Jeddah. The night before there had been reports about Jonestown on the BBC but the tragic conclusion still wasn't fully known then. It was now. The old man stared at me with implacable eyes. He wanted an answer.

My Arabic has never been close to fluent but during those years in Jeddah it was barely passable. I gave it my best shot and said, "Jimmy Jones. Jimmy Jones is *majnoon*, crazy."

He replied, "*Majnoon*?"

"Yes. *Majnoon*. There was a *shaitan*, devil, in his heart, *galb*."

"A *shaitan* in his heart?"

He blinked at me. "*Majnoon*?"

I nodded solemnly.

He considered this and then said, "*Khalas*, finished. Jimmee Jones *majnoon*." As if to say that all Americans weren't insane, it was only Jimmy Jones who was nuts. He gave me a grin that showed all five of his remaining teeth, turned around and started up the cab.

His name was Abu Hamid. Even compensating for the wear and tear of Bedouin life, Abu Hamid was fairly old, maybe even 70, and had happily spent his entire life in the desert north of Jeddah. His son Hamid had died as a

Abu Hamid ~ 103

young boy, he had three daughters and many camels. His wife had fallen ill and needed to be treated every week at the hospital, so he had moved to Jeddah and was getting by driving a taxi.

He really didn't like the city. Pointing at the trash along the road he said, "The city is dirty. In the desert, every wind makes it clean again." He couldn't wait to return to his camels.

He asked if I had a son. When I said I had a son and a daughter, he said "Congratulations! Two." And then added that I should get with the program and have at least four more sons. We had a fine ride. He dropped me at the airport, and I watched as he crabbed his Datsun past a double-parked Mercedes limousine to drive away.

I could well have been the only American he had ever talked to, so he was right to be wary of picking up Jimmy Jones II as cab fare. However, like a true Bedouin, he was insatiably curious and felt it was his right to stop and ask me point blank about Jonestown. I'm sure that in his many years in the desert he had met his share of mentally disturbed people. Maybe even witnessed the devil jumping into the heart of someone he knew closely. When his glacial expression turned into a near-toothless grin we were no longer a young American and an ancient Arabian, we were two guys going to the airport.

Flying to Riyadh, looking down at the desert that might have been part of his range, I kept thinking about Abu Hamid. Born around 1910, in his lifetime he would witness the end of generations of tribal conflicts swept away by the sword of King Abdul Aziz ibn Saud. He could finally roam peacefully with his camels. And then the beginning of the end of his entire way of life when the first pick-up trucks appeared in the desert. Now he was driving around Jeddah in a beat-up taxi, listening to the radio, apparently intrigued about the news of Americans and their inexplicable behavior.

Watching the desert unfold beneath me, its surface marked by alluvial fans and river beds that once ran wild and free five thousand years ago, now dried up like the wrinkles on the old man's face, I realized that Abu Hamid was more sophisticated than the average American.

Bitter civil wars and terrible massacres in Africa, devastating famines in Bangladesh, horrendous ferry boat disasters in Indonesia, earthquakes in Italy or bloody coups in Chile barely entered the American consciousness. A few years later 7,000 Indians would be killed in one night by the negligent operation of a Union Carbide pesticide manufacturing plant in Bhopal and it barely registered on an American public immersed in wondering, "Who shot JR?"

During the student demonstrations of the 60s, the protestors would chant, "The whole world is watching." And it was. Unfortunately, neither then nor now do many Americans seem to be watching the world as closely as Abu Hamid is watching them.

MEA 747 at the Singapore airport. Photo by Andrew Hunt

SPECIAL TECHNIQUES

Readers of my various stories will know by now that I have a fondness for special techniques. The planning and tactics I applied at the age of six to procure grape Jell-O from the highest cabinet in the kitchen was perfectly executed only to end in ruin. When I came back into the house with vermillion lips and a mouthful of purple teeth to say, "Hi Mom," I busted myself.

On the other hand, my success in playing hooky for a month in Kindergarten was a triumph of tradecraft. However, the satisfaction that I felt in devising one of my most brilliant maneuvers evaporated when I found myself in the presence of a master.

It was two days before the Haj began in 1978. Against all my instincts for self-preservation I had chosen to do some business in Riyadh and was now trying to get home to Jeddah, knowing full well that more than a million Muslims were headed my way too. I expected at least a tenth of them would be in the departure hall. I was wrong by several orders of magnitude. There were only about a thousand. But I wasn't wrong about the fervor and excitement in the room.

The departure hall was one giant room about 80 feet long and half as wide with 30-foot ceilings. A floor-to-ceiling glass wall enclosed the side facing the runway. A half-dozen glass doors marked the different loading gates. I figured that I'd arrive two hours early to get a good position in the line but when I walked into the lounge I realized that there were at least six plane-loads of people waiting to fly. Some passengers had missed their connecting flight, many of them were the victims of enthusiastic over-booking, some were flying to another destination and more than a few of them seemed to just be wandering around without any apparent purpose.

A huge room populated by Muslims from all over the world is quite a sight. Besides hundreds of Saudis in white thobes and variegated ghuttras there are Omanis in yellow and green turbans, stately Nigerians in dashikis, Bosnians in worn-out pea-coats, Filipinos in brilliant pastel Dacron shirts, Tunisians in three-piece suits, it is a full palette of global fashion.

The overhead PA system, completely incomprehensible but loud, echoes around the room while everyone is talking at the same time; frustrated, impatient but mostly excited to be going to Mecca on the Haj. Of course my objective is somewhat less devout. I just want to see my wife and kids.

People are wall to wall and about 20 feet deep from the gates. Half of them are already waving their boarding passes. A foot taller than most everybody, I'm a highly conspicuous American and there is no way that I can discretely make my way through this teeming crowd pretending to be a *Haji*.

I decide to improvise a special technique and flatten my back against the left wall and slowly make my way forward. I have two hours so I am able to glacially proceed undetected. Or so I thought.

When I reach the glass wall and turn to inch along its face someone bumps into me. I spin to see a short, mid-twenties Iranian with three chins and a marvelous pot belly wearing a faded, green hounds-tooth sport coat. He flashes me a grin and says, "I see you. You go. Then I go."

Delighted that he has recognized my stratagem I reach out my hand and say, "My name is Tim. What's yours? We go."

Shaking my hand he says, "Me Badr. We go."

And we went.

Slinking our way along the glass wall I had to decide which of the six gates would be our destination. Most of the planes seemed to be parked on the runway to the left of the wall and primal instinct told me that the hall's Feng Shui tended to flow left, so the closest gates would be One, Two and Three. The obvious choice was Gate Two.

If we were lucky. we'd have a clear shot at Two, yet we could quickly pivot to insinuate ourselves into the flanking gates. So I lead us against the wall to make our way to just to the left of Gate Two. We talk for a bit.

Badr grew up in Shiraz and moved to work as a clerk for the oil company in Bandar Abbas where he learned some English. He didn't like the town much and moved home to work in his family's tile business. He had just married, his wife was pregnant and this Haj was as much for his child as for himself. As he told me, "I don't care boy or girl. I want strong. May God breathe on him ... or her."

Waiting, we all watch the movements of the gate attendants closer than Gordon Gekko watched the Dow Jones. Earlier I had noticed a particular duo and search the crowd for them. Fierce-looking, bearded men, dressed in pantaloons and long gabardine shirts under vests, their heads covered with those distinctive flat, woolen hats wrapped in drab turbans, they are George and Lennie from Steinbeck's *Of Mice and Men* – straight out of the mountains of Afghanistan. The smaller man, George, is built like a whippet – lean and rangy, with a sharp face and small, busy eyes. Lennie is a giant. At least 6 feet 6 and almost 300 pounds, his craggy face and bushy eyebrows dully scan the crowd, either looking for danger or prey or just totally confused by the multitudes around him. It was pretty obvious who was the brains of this operation.

Choosing the direct approach, the Afghani duo has waded directly through the middle of the crowd, George drafting in Lennie's wake. Who is going to object to a 300 pound Afghani? They were now stopped about 5 feet from Gate One by the sheer crush of humanity. Now everybody is chattering and waving their boarding pass above their heads. Ozone like you might feel just before a thunderstorm breaks fills the room as two senior officials squeeze through the crowd to the front of the hall. They huddle up with the now clearly nervous gate attendants.

Their technique for dealing with these thousand travellers is absolutely brilliant. After the huddle breaks an attendant walks to each gate and goes through the motions of getting ready to open. The attention of the crowd is now immediately split in sixths. When the attendant at Gate Six acknowledges that he is ready, Badr pokes me in the back and says, "Run."

Before I can even acknowledge Badr, the agent at Gate One opens the door and a thousand people lunge forward as dozens of lucky passengers burst onto the runway. The hapless ticket agent throws up his hands and doesn't even try to collect boarding passes. With some mild jostling Badr and I make it out the door to join the 100 meter dash to the gleaming Middle East Airlines 747 in the distance.

At first everyone tries to be cool about it and walk quickly, but less than ten yards from the gate we break into a run and the race is on. I see a jowly Bahraini pearl merchant in tasseled Italian shoes run faster than he has in his entire life – a personal best. A trim, big-jawed Kuwaiti businessman at the other side of the pack is holding his own until the handle of his briefcase fails and the case explodes open on the tarmac to send his papers into the wind. At one point a diminutive, grey-haired older man with a meticulously starched thobe, laced guffiyeh and gold Cross pens in his top pocket hitches up his thobe and smokes two lean Eritreans in flip-flops to advance to the head of the pack. A burly Iraqi who had been the first one through Gate One starts to fade twenty meters out. I'm doing fine. Loping along, not yet running. In a moving crowd it's always better to be on the flanks. If the crowd stacks up you won't be trampled and if necessary you can speed up at the end and work yourself into the front.

I look for Badr but don't see him because he is right behind me. His cheerful face is red and sweaty but he is game enough to motor that belly across the runway. "Run!" he says. A sturdy Sudanese in a mechanic's jumpsuit and work boots comes pounding out of nowhere and takes a lead. We reach the landing steps and form into line. I figure Badr and I are about the fortieth or so passengers in line.

We ascend to the rear door of the 747 to be met by a beatific vision, the senior steward of the plane. A handsome, mid-thirties Lebanese of medium height, slim with broad shoulders, smooth-shaven with a haircut so perfect it looks as if he has just came from the barber. I'll call him Emile.

In his immaculate, perfectly-tailored uniform he meets each passenger as if he is meeting a long-lost cousin. His wide smile is a genetic gift from his Phoenician ancestors but his utter coolness is self-taught. Confusion and chaos have surrounded every aspect of this flight but Emile is as relaxed as if he were sipping Campari on the Corniche in Nice. This is obviously not his first rodeo.

The last third of the plane is already occupied so I hurry up to the front, rush into a window seat and immediately pretend that I am sleeping. This is the well-known and always reliable hedgehog defense. The theory being that the stewards are less likely to evict someone sleeping in a window seat when the person in the aisle seat is so much easier prey. This tactic becomes unnecessary when Badr slips in next to me and the hefty Sudanese mechanic takes the aisle.

We are all on edge and none of us will be safe until the plane leaves the ground. As the seats fill up Emile works his way to the front of the plane directing traffic. The last seat is taken when he spots the two Afghanis: a very suspicious George and the glowering, hunched-over giant lumbering down the aisle. Lennie is muttering loudly to himself. Everyone in the plane senses the impending conflict. Immediately Emile breaks into a thousand volt smile and gestures to them, "My friends I have been waiting for you. Please come forward."

They look warily at him but Emile laughs and waves them forward. "I have been waiting for you. This plane is so crowded. Here. Come up here, I have another airplane waiting for you. It is so much stronger. I only wish that I could fly on it. Come right through here." He is so convincing that I'm almost ready to give up my own seat.

George and Lennie relax and smile at their good fortune. Emile shakes each man's hand as he ushers them out the front door to the stronger airplane, then quickly closes the hatch and pulls down the locking lever. He pauses to straighten his tie and turns to the cabin to take a half bow as we all break into wild applause. The master has just given us a lesson in the proper practice of special techniques.

One and One Makes Four

THE DOUBLE-SHOT SOLUTION

With Lou Reed's passing and so many observers discussing his impact on the contemporary culture of the 60s I can't stop thinking about the first time I ever heard the Velvet Underground. It was in Dhahran when I was 19. This very wonderful but basically quiet girl, I'll call Sharon, who I had known my whole life finally had convinced her parents to let her have a small party for only her college-age friends – as if that was more respectable than the usual horde of returning students.

The day before the party she asked me if I would be the bar tender. This was obviously the worst decision possible but I was touched that she thought I was worthy of such a responsibility and of course I was at her service. So the next night I arrived early in a clean shirt, perfectly happy to be a proper bar tender. She appeared in an old faded blue men's Oxford shirt tied at her midriff and cut off blue-jeans. This was a different side of Sharon. I didn't see her much at other parties and presumed she was a stay at home girl. I was obviously wrong. Anyway she showed me her parents' bar set-up and put out the ingredients, the mixers - Pepsi, Miranda or Schweppes, the shot glass and the classic Aramco wax cups.

Well this wasn't my first cocktail party but my problem with the previous ones was that after waiting in line, you'd get your one shot and it wasn't long before you'd have to wait in line again.

My brilliant insight was that I'd give each drinker a double-shot and then I wouldn't have to see him or her for twice as long. It was a great idea. There were about 30 college-age kids and things were boiling along when some guy came rushing through the front door with the Velvet Underground album, the one with the banana on the cover. "This is so cool." he says. And it was.

There goes the Stones and that record starts playing for about the first time in Arabia. The party was already cooking pretty well but then the cacophonous Velvets started up, dead pan Nico's voice came in and Lou Reed began his hypnotic droning that somehow became so urgent, everybody was dancing and chanting lyrics that they had never heard before. That girl from Ras Tanura who was a junior at the University of Florida fell to the floor and started doing the Dirty Gator with her boyfriend.

Half a dozen kids were bunched together like a stalk of asparagus with their arms up in the air undulating like a gigantic sea anemone. Strange James was in an air guitar paroxysm and everyone else was just flailing it up.

And there was supposedly quiet Sharon doing a wild Scissors dance with Barclay from Abqaiq.

By the time that *Waiting for the Man* started playing the whole room was a writhing bacchanalia of frenzied dancers that went on and on until they collapsed in exhaustion when the record ended.

A new album went on the turntable but no one had any more to give. Listless, worn out, couples started to leave and barely three hours later, inexplicably, this party was just about over. An old friend of mine who I'd known since second grade, came up for a drink. I poured her the usual double-shots I'd been serving all night long, when she said, "Do you know that is a double-shot glass?"

Yikes! I had been pouring quadruple shots.

Can't say if that had something to do with the enthusiasm for the Velvet Underground but it was directly responsible for the short half-life of the party. I closed the bar and fled. The next day Sharon called to thank me for my help. She couldn't stop talking about the Velvets. To her the party was a fabulous success and thanks to Lou Reed I guess it was.

I didn't ask about Barclay from Abqaiq.

A famous landmark along the Airport Road in Riyadh – 1974
"Turn left at the wrecked pick-up truck."

WELCOME TO RIYADH

In the 1970s the airports in Saudi Arabia were actually near their cities. Dhahran International was at the air base a few miles from camp. The Riyadh and Jeddah airports were right in town with their entrances just off the street. After the price of oil quadrupled in 1973, Riyadh was awash in Petrodollars and deluged with thousands of businessmen, contractors, consultants, carpet baggers and schemers from all over the world who had absolutely no idea of what to expect when they landed. This made for a particularly target-rich environment for the hoteliers and cab drivers of the city.

Consider a neophyte. Call him Leland Martin Dunlop III, a bond salesman from Scarsdale, New York, who arrives on Middle East Airlines, MEA, at Riyadh International in the summer of 1974. Planning to make a multi-million dollar deal, Leland is dressed for success in a blue wool suit wearing a crisp, white shirt with French cuffs, dark-blue onyx cuff links, and a red power-tie as he steps out of the plane into a torrid 120-degree furnace made hotter by acres of tarmac radiating visible heat waves. He walks down the landing steps and across the asphalt to the terminal entrance where 10 feet from the building the passengers are delayed by a portly Syrian caught up in some heated disagreement with the lanky guard at the door. After an interminable wait in the direct sun Leland's face starts to flush and he's beginning to think that maybe the blue wool suit wasn't the best fashion choice.

Finally and inexplicably the portly man starts laughing, shakes hands with the smiling guard, moves on and Leland enters the terminal where four lines await a special kind of hell called Immigration and Passport Control. Line three looks the shortest so he takes his place, silently estimating that he'll be through in fifteen minutes. Leland uses the husky Syrian who's standing in line four to compare his relative progress. He's already two places ahead of the man by being in the shorter line three. He wonders why the Syrian has passed on this obvious advantage. Ten minutes go by and Leland advances one place as does the Syrian. This won't be too bad he thinks and then the distinguished looking Egyptian at the head of line three calls off to his right and a wife, four children and two ancient nannies join him.

Forty five minutes later the Syrian is gone and Leland is still motionless. There seems to be some problem with the Egyptian's papers. Leland's highly-polished black

Oxford shoes bought last week at Brooks Brothers for the trip were a little tight to begin with but now the leather has each foot in a vise-like grip that is steadily tightening. Standing on the hard terrazzo floor, his arches are falling faster than his patience when the Egyptian family finally clears. The three Filipinos ahead in line are easily processed and then the passport man closes his cage.

What?

Leland was only one place away and now hope has evaporated. He mills about in front of the closed station muttering to himself until a guard comes over to move him on to the back of line four. Unfortunately a planeload of Korean workers has just arrived so line four is now so long that it stretches back out of the terminal into the sun. Leland takes off his blue wool jacket and looks for a pebble that he can suck on to keep hydrated.

Before it's over Leland has made a bandanna out of his monogrammed handkerchief, his tie is loosened and his shirt, soaked with sweat, is unbuttoned to his sternum. He has lost both cuff links. Nearly two hours later he is awkwardly holding his Oxfords and briefcase in one hand, the passport in the other, when he walks up in his socks to the customs officer.

While talking to a friend standing behind him, the sharply-uniformed, twenty-five-year old inspector takes Leland's passport, glances at him for five seconds, stamps the entry visa and turns back to his friend. Elapsed time of the transaction is fourteen seconds. That was smooth enough, maybe Leland's luck is turning which of course is impossible. Now he must enter into the inner-most level of Leland's Dantean nightmare. It's called the Customs Hall.

Leland walks into a room about as big as a gymnasium furnished with half a dozen steel inspection tables about 20 feet long and hundreds of people from practically every country on earth, from all stations of life, shouting dozens of languages at the same time. The acoustics are so bad that all the voices blend into a low roar punctuated by the occasional screech. Every second person is smoking a cigarette, and Leland feels his asthma coming on. All around are gigantic piles of luggage ranging from elegant hat boxes and handsome Italian leather suitcases to cardboard boxes bound with twine, gaily-painted tin trunks from Pakistan and rolled bundles of bedding. Someone has a bird cage with two bright-blue parrots.

Even though Leland has spent nearly three hours in passport control his plane hasn't yet unloaded. He knows this because his wife Polly smartly suggested that he tag his bags with yellow ribbons and he doesn't see them. Killing time Leland takes in the crowd, marveling even at the myriad nationalities surrounding him: Algerians, Brazilians, Nigerians, Jordanians, Germans, Indonesians, Koreans, Qataris, Lebanese, Australians, Sudanese, Malaysians and many more than he can possibly identify.

In his whole life he has only known Americans except for some Swedish exchange students he met one college summer. Mostly white Americans. He could count on his fingers the amount of any given group of non-white Americans: African-Americans, Hispanics, Asians, Native Americans, he knows by name. If he'd stayed in Arabia long enough he might have eventually realized that to the rest of the world regardless of race they're all Americans. The differences between them being trivial compared to their similarity.

The customs inspectors seem to be somewhat haphazard. Meticulously examining a beat-up beige Samsonite and passing unopened a huge bundle of something or other. They aren't wearing any uniforms, just the white thobe and red checkered guttrah. Porters are running in every direction. At another line an angry inspector makes a skinny Yemeni empty his duffel bag full of oranges that spill off the table to roll around the floor in all directions. Beyond the glass wall of the customs hall a boiling mass of people are assembled to meet the new arrivals.

Oh, there's an agent from MEA. Leland is in luck. He doesn't have to wait anymore. His luggage is lost.

Filling out the lost baggage report with the young Lebanese agent, Leland says the bags can be identified by the yellow ribbons that Polly put on them. The agent stops writing, looks up at Leland and says, "Yellow tags are used to flag baggage for secondary disease control. If your bags arrive tomorrow, they will be inspected and fumigated. That should only take two days. Check back with me in four days."

Leland is stunned. Like the time he got hit squarely between the eyes by a handball while playing down at the club. In a daze, he leaves customs to push into a whirling circus of people crowding the exit. Waiting for their friends and family, Turks shout across the room to each other, Somalis cluster into chattering groups that block the way. Women in black purdah wave madly to some relative in the customs hall. Yemenis skitter around trying to snag bags, babies scream, and dozens of men in white thobes wander around aimlessly. Leland regroups. He forces his shoes back on his swollen feet, tying them real loosely this time. He runs his fingers through his sweat-matted hair, puts on his jacket, straightens his tie, throws his shoulders back and steps out of the terminal. He is ready to do business.

The driveway is lined with taxis, mostly yellow Datsuns that have been wounded in one fender or the other. The drivers are clustered together. They see Leland and there is some kind of huddle before a lean, middle-aged Bedouin who looks like a well-groomed pirate approaches. He fixes Leland with his dark brown eyes and says, "Sabeak English."

Before he can realize how stupid he sounds, Leland says, "Why yes, I do speak English." Then he laughs to himself because it isn't a question.

The cab driver doesn't laugh and says, "Where you go?"

Leland looks at his itinerary and replies, "The Sahari Palace."

"Three hundred fifty riyals."

Leland thinks a hundred dollars is a lot for a cab ride. But then this is a boom town. And he's had it and just wants to get to his room. That's probably about right. Maybe it's even a deal. "Here's your money, let's go."

The cab driver folds up the money, breaks into a faint grin and says "Okay, okay. Me Ali."

Ali is a little bewildered that there is no luggage but he pries open the bashed-in door, and Leland slides into the back seat. He can't wait to take a hot bath and get a good nap. Ali fires up the Datsun, drives fifty yards to the boulevard, and amid honking horns and screeching brakes recklessly dashes directly across the onrushing traffic in both directions to deliver Leland Martin Dunlop III to the Sahari Palace. Elapsed time: two minutes at fifty dollars a minute.

Beaten, weary and totally confused, Leland walks into the hotel thanking God that his ordeal is over. It's not a very impressive place. The sparse landscaping seems to be indifferently maintained and the paint over the entrance is peeling but he doesn't care. He has survived the gauntlet. He has a reservation.

Behind the reception desk a thin, sharply-dressed Pakistani clerk with thick, well-gelled black hair welcomes him in the Queen's English and cheerfully scans the reservations list only to announce that Leland's name is not on it. Of course this couldn't be true, and Leland rifles through his briefcase to proudly produce the letter confirming his reservation and two hundred dollar deposit. The clerk scrutinizes the letter, hands it back to Leland and then shifts his comprehension of the English language into low gear to say, "Not signed."

Leland starts babbling about what his travel agent in Manhattan told him, about the telexes he sent and so on as the clerk nods his head in faint agreement, though apparently he has no idea what the American is saying. When Leland finishes his soliloquy the Pakistani says, "No rooms."

Desperate by now Leland pleads with the clerk, throws himself at his pity. He absolutely has to clean himself up for a vital meeting that night with his contact, the cousin of the personal secretary to the second assistant-deputy of the minister. It's bad enough that his luggage is lost, he hasn't slept for two days, he is seriously dehydrated and his business will collapse if he misses this appointment. He has two children in private school and a wife who shops at I. Magnin and Saks Fifth Avenue. They will starve. The clerk looks back with great sympathy and says, "No rooms."

Crestfallen and devoid of hope, Leland is a broken man on the verge of a total nervous breakdown when the Pakistani with impeccable timing clears his throat and says, "However."

And that is how Leland Martin Dunlop III, the esteemed bond salesman from New York city, became the proud resident of the lumpy, red velour, imitation Louis the 16th sofa in the lobby of the Sahari Palace Hotel for the bargain price of nine hundred riyals a night.

Dhahran Recreation Complex -1949

THE RULE OF LIFE

As far back as I can remember the fundamental rule of life was to never walk along a street when an alley was available. The alleys of Dhahran offered so many advantages that Milt and I could never figure why the adults didn't use them too.

The alleys were narrow enough that they were shadier, and looking into backyards was a lot more intriguing than the manicured front yards. Some backyards were like English gardens, some were nothing but a lawn bordered with hedges, and others lay bare and neglected with a half assembled motorcycle on the patio. Guys stored their boats and hobby cars in the back and some people built garden sheds and workshops along the back fence.

Every back yard had two industrial-strength clothesline poles made of 2-inch steel pipes welded into a T with holes drilled along the crossbar to thread the clothesline through. Painted in industrial-grade silver, in Arabia they dried your clothes in ten minutes. They were also terrific impromptu targets for pellet guns but that's another story.

And of course the alleys offered the freedom from adult supervision. Almost complete anonymity. There was no chance that the nosey Mrs. Almquist would drive by, catch you screwing around and mix the news into her relentless gossip machine. You could smoke a purloined L&M cigarette in safety.

The alley itself was paved and lined with treasure chests in the shape of the 55 gallon oil barrels that Aramco used as trash cans. In the 50s, Dhahran was a resource poor environment. Khobar still wasn't fully developed, and products, especially American goods, weren't readily available, so the men hoarded screws and nuts, car parts, metal stock, lumber and tools to barter among themselves. The women collected fabric, traded dress patterns and shared their recipes and dishware while we alley rats acquired and savored exquisite pieces of junk we discovered in the trash.

Find a couple of fluorescent tubes and we would instantly have a dramatic and very brief sword fight that ended in a burst of shattered glass and a faint cloud of super-carcinogenic mist. Milt once found the broken front end of a trombone and spent the rest of the day blowing into the bare end until his lips bled. If you were real lucky you might find a tattered issue of some True Crime magazine with bold headlines and lurid pictures. Readers may remember the time that Cecil found some nudie playing cards in an alley.

There were treasures to be found. We'd grab stuff and move on. After a while we'd lose interest in a broken toaster or something, discard it along the way and the rest of the stuff we'd lug home. Milt and I were self-styled scavenger kings

When we were about 11, we both got crystal radio sets. They were the most basic sort of radio setup, so simple that a kid could assemble it and so magical that it was a gateway device into electronics. Milt and I became crazed with electronics and fascinated with the multitude of tubes, the rainbow colors and distinctive shapes of the ceramic diodes, resistors and capacitors. We had no idea how these things worked but we knew they had power.

So we started collecting them which wasn't too hard because we knew the alley behind the radio shop, an entire building dedicated to Aramco's extensive communications department. These were the days before the transistor when radios operated on tubes and equipment could actually be repaired by human beings, so the radio shop trash cans overflowed with hundreds of feet of wire and boxes of defective or expired components from tubes to button switches. We hauled away enough parts to stock a Radio Shack but we still didn't know what they did.

There was a radio club in Dhahran of a dozen junior high kids and a wonderful middle-aged Ham radio enthusiast as adviser, so we went to a meeting. It was a disaster. We were a couple of years younger than everyone else and entirely ignorant.

The star of the group was a ninth-grade Brainiac surrounded by a few devotees. Curtis really knew his stuff. He came over to talk to us and quickly discovered that Milt didn't know the difference between an ohm and a millivolt. Thirteen-year-olds can be particularly cruel, and Curtis turned on us, mocked us and dripped disdain all over us in front of his posse. The rest of the meeting we sat dejected in the back, smoldering in resentment and shame at our ignorance.

But our enthusiasm wasn't dampened and the next day we scored two boxes of tubes and a power supply from behind the radio shop. We chattered about Ham radios and went to the library to stare at incomprehensible diagrams that might as well have been hieroglyphics.

Every day I'd meet Milt on 10th Street and we would walk to school on 3rd Street. The alleys were perpendicular to our route so we took the sidewalk. Between 6th Street and 3rd Street there was a traffic circle around an air-conditioning plant that formed a choke point.

Every day we passed a red Aramco Dodge truck parked at the curb. We couldn't help but notice that there were two Motorola portable radios about the size of thick, long brief-cases propped up against the passenger seat. Just lying there. Day after day we walked by, probably the guy who drove that truck worked nights. Look the door is unlocked again.

We were unable to resist. If they wouldn't tell us how to make the things, we would borrow a couple of working radios and possess the power of the air waves. So we devised a plan.

Aramco operated its own transcontinental airline until the advent of the Boeing 707 and in the process created the iconic Aramco bag. A heavy-vinyl carry-on satchel emblazoned with the Aramco logo, it was given to every Aramcon going on long leave. The green bag became a universally recognized badge of kinship throughout the airports of the world. It was readily available, and did I tell you that it was just large enough to contain a complete Motorola 20 pound portable radio?

It's about 3 in the afternoon, 113 in the shade, when Milt and I stroll towards the red Dodge Power Wagon parked across the street from the AC plant. To keep the truck cool, the windows were half down. The keys were in the ignition and the doors were unlocked. We take a deep breath, open the passenger door, scoop up the radios and jam them into our Aramco bags.

They fit perfectly. Except for the 4-foot-long whip antenna. Fumbling around on the sidewalk, we snake the antenna out and then bend it back into the bag, close the truck door and scurry across into the alley. Now we are two kids walking along with Aramco bags, completely inconspicuous save for the curving antenna blooming from the bag. At one point, Milt's antenna slips out and snaps to its full height. We think this is hilarious.

Absolutely safe in the anonymous alleys, we work our way home. About halfway, we run into the only form of life that exists in these mean streets – another kid. Henry is messing around in his back yard working on his soap box race car and sees us pass. He is a couple of years younger than us, a good enough kid if a bit simple, but we give him a hearty greeting and press on with our clandestine mission.

At 10th Street we split up and I go into the central air-conditioning room built into the side of every house. I hide the radio behind the giant condensing unit and nonchalantly walk into the house. My sisters are baking cookies with my mom, my brother is practicing the piano. I exchange pleasantries and then split for the phone in the hallway.

"Hey Milt. How are you doing? Are you ready? Good. I'll sign on in ten minutes." Milt and I synchronize our watches, cheap timepieces with the face of King Saud that we bought for five riyals each in Khobar. We saw that technique in countless war movies, so we knew what to do.

Milt and I are a classic example of the adage that a little information is dangerous ... and also utterly useless. Again from watching too many spy movies, we know that when using a radio transmitter the Nazis could triangulate that signal, pinpoint the transmitter and it was Kaput! So we have to keep our traffic brief. We also know that we have to use code names. I power up the Motorola.

"Come in Lizard Head. Do you hear me?"

"Come in Jellyfish. Loud and clear."

"Roger that, Lizard Head. How are you doing?"

"Great. I hear you clearly Jellyfish. Can you hear me?"

"You're fading, Milt. I mean Lizard Head. Can you read me?"

"Jellyfish, I can hear you."

"Lizard Head, you are clear. So do you think Lana really likes me?"

"Yes, she likes you Jellyfish. As much as she likes juicy, green hedge caterpillars."

"Thanks loads, Lizard Head. We better go before they catch us. I'll call you on the phone. Ten four, over and out."

"Ten four, over and out."

And cleverly, we sign off before the radio detection units can hunt us down. I then call Milt on the phone and we talk at length about our career as underground wireless warriors.

Over the next few days we exchanged thirty-second bursts on the radios and then spent hours on the phone dissecting our radio technique. The funniest part was that we had the phone and didn't really need the walkie-talkies but they possessed a magic the phone couldn't touch.

We had a great friend named Wilkins who was dying to join our network so I gave him my radio. He took it away in an Aramco bag. I figured that I had now washed my hands of the original heist as possession is nine-tenths of a guilty verdict. Wilkins and Milt communicated in thirty-second bursts and then called me to discuss the salient details. Milt found a scorpion in the hiding place in his AC room and Wilkins said a famous four-letter word over the air waves. Our secret network was humming along and all was good.

Four days later the three of us were called out of sixth-grade art class. We were marched in silence to the principal's office and separated from each other. I was brought into a bare room with two chairs facing each other across a table. The only thing missing was a bright interrogation light to shine into my face. In one of the chairs sat Mr. Bricklin, the head of all of Aramco's industrial security. He was a veteran police department officer from New Jersey who maybe had a few years with the FBI. He gave me a withering look as if I had been rolling old ladies in Asbury Park and told me to sit down. It must be a lot of fun to sweat out a confession from an 11-year-old.

He told me that each radio cost five thousand dollars, which in those days was like twenty thousand.

In America that was felony grand theft, good for some sentence just short of the electric chair. In my case, I would go to reform school until I was 18 and, though he didn't say it, become an accomplished and very well informed criminal. Then he said that my dad, who was a highly placed executive at Aramco, could lose his job because of my perfidy.

As if I didn't know it, he casually managed to mention that in the Kingdom they cut off the hands of thieves. I'm stressing out and desperately, in a weak voice, play my only card. "I don't have any radio. Search the AC closet at my house." Oops.

Bricklin broke into a cold, tight smile and hissed, "I know that you and Milt used Aramco bags."

Busted. I would strangle Henry. I returned Bricklin's steely gaze, a sharp look honed to a razor edge by dueling with hundreds of hardened criminals, and started crying. My dad was going to lose his job because of me.

Next, an overwrought Bricklin broke down Milt and Wilkins until he had the case of the missing walkie-talkies all tied up and delivered to management with a bow. What Milt and I didn't know and never could have imagined was the reason for Bricklin's panic.

At that time there were a variety of liberation movements within the Gulf, the Dhofari Liberation Front in Oman being the most prominent. One of these groups with a couple of Aramco-frequency portable radios could get up to all kinds of mischief. The loss of these radios was a major breach of security and Bricklin was sweating it – silently contemplating who might quickly buy his sail boat before he was fired and deported. It must have altered his life to find out that the culprits weren't a hardened cell of exiled Emarati separatists but rather a trio of misguided, sub-adolescent radio geeks.

The fallout from this caper was enormous. All of society came down on us. Though we were 11, somehow we had ruined our fathers' careers; we were thieves, felons, Juvenile Delinquents. We weren't allowed to talk to each other, we couldn't go to recreation for at least a decade and in my case basically everyone except the gardener was "disappointed" in me. I was crushed, defeated and guilt-ridden. I turned into an obsequious, pudgy little goodie-goodie, a kid that I would have loathed six months before.

Life moves on, but so too does remorse. Contemplating our crime I began to think that Milt and I had done a great service to Aramco. Now all the radios would be more secure, or at least the windows rolled up and the truck doors locked. We were security consultants so to speak. I also knew that the law in Arabia was that if a man left his window down, his door unlocked and a bag of coins on the passenger seat, he was the criminal for tempting the thief. I was a Sharia law scholar before I even knew what it meant. We took good care of the radios, kept them in an air-conditioned environment and only turned them on for two minutes a day. It wasn't such a terrible thing we did commandeering two walkie-talkies for the Jellyfish Liberation Front of Dhahran.

AKA Jellyfish, Industrial Security Consultant at 11

After a couple of months the contrition started to wear off too. I was being so good that I was boring myself to death and decided to return to the Rule of Life. I started roaming the alleys again. One day I happened to be walking up the alley between Eleventh and Twelfth Streets towards the swimming pool, the Fiesta Room and the rest of the forbidden zone, when I saw Milt duck into the head of the alley and hide behind a garbage can. An Aramco security car drove by. It was dramatic but I'm certain that the driver couldn't have cared less about some kid crouching in the alley. I whistled to Milt and we met up.

Aside from school we hadn't seen too much of each other. He was scouting the perimeter of the recreation block for ways to sneak in. Of course we didn't know that everyone in Dhahran had completely forgotten all about our caper and we are free to go bowling, to the movies, swimming, to the Fiesta Room. No one cared.

In the back yard of a house on that alley an old African berry tree of some sort flourished. It must have been planted in the Forties, as it was more than 2 feet in diameter at the trunk and 30 feet tall. About 8 feet up, a foot-thick branch projected perfectly perpendicular from the trunk for about 5 feet before bending upward and a little over the back fence into the alley. We'd climb up the tree, scoot onto the limb and chatter like lemurs. We named it after the famous blimp, the Flying Cigar, which is where Milt and I adjourned to discuss our options.

In season, the Flying Cigar was covered with berries of some sort, red-golden fruit, maybe the size of cherries, that were heavenly sweet. However, it was difficult to discern between a ripe berry and a non-ripe. We were always wary because if you bit into a non-ripe you were doomed. It had a wretched bitterness, and your whole mouth puckered up like you had swallowed a handful of chalk dust. So Milt and I talked on the tree limb.

We agreed that maybe electronics wasn't our destiny but we'd find something else and remain allies in life. We each grabbed a berry and swore our friendship. We'd eat the whole berry regardless of how it tasted. We popped them into our mouths, bit down and tasted the sweetest berries in all of Arabia.

So a few days later, I'm at Milt's house in the afternoon. It's perfect. His parents are gone and there is no adult within a thousand yards. Milt's room is decorated with his artifacts and discoveries. There is a deeply dented, steel hard-hat, a partially intact umbrella, a mangled road cone, a cracked green salt-tablet dispenser and of course the loot from behind the radio shop: A big cardboard box filled with a spaghetti nest of colored wires, buckets of radio tubes, and shoe boxes filled with switches, knobs and the pretty ceramic components that are color banded with wire leads at each end. We can't help but run our fingers through the box of resistors and diodes that contain a secret that we'll never know.

Then Milt says, "Look at this! I just found it in the alley behind Miller's house." He goes under his bed and pulls out a large cast-aluminum cylinder maybe 3 feet long and about 10 inches in diameter. There's an electrical plug on one end. At the middle of the cylinder is a kind of foot-wide scoop-type cowling that flares out about 6 inches from the tube. It is an industrial cylindrical fan whose blades run lengthwise to blow air out of the scoop and onto to some critical piece of equipment. He couldn't wait to show it to me. The fan weighed about 20 pounds and was covered in oily grime that apparently Milt didn't notice when he dropped it on the white Chenille bedspread. He plugged in the fan and it hummed to life, pushing out a steady blast of air. It was cool in all ways.

But after a few minutes it was still a fan, so Milt, always the empirical scientist, says, "Let's see what happens?" and picks up a ceramic capacitor the size of the tip of your little finger and tosses it into the scoop. There is this rattling sound from the fan as the component ricochets around within the housing and then comes spitting right back at us with the velocity of a Sandy Koufax fastball. It hits Milt right in the elbow and he howls in pain. I break out laughing. This is the funniest thing we've ever done. Milt throws in three small resistors, they clink around for a bit and then blast out like a shotgun and I get stung in the knee cap.

Standing against the far wall pitching small components into the fan cannon, we are having the time of our lives dodging flying shrapnel. We both wear glasses and most of the debris comes in at mid-torso to the knees, so to us this is a perfectly safe and acceptable activity. The thing about the fan was that if you got in closer to make your throw easier that fifty-ohm resistor would come flying out faster than you could dodge. What could be more enjoyable?

We feed the fan for at least twenty minutes when Milt realizes that we have run out of components to pitch. He thinks for a moment and then brightens into a Eureka moment and says, "I have this." He triumphantly pulls a cigar box off the shelf. It is filled with 2-inch stove bolts, nuts and washers. Perfect.

I toss in a washer. It clinks around in the fan and it clinks around some more before it fires. By some coincidence of nature the washer sails out in an arc like a Frisbee and clips the side of Milt's glasses. Nothing could be better. The stakes are raised and the game is on. I have so much fun throwing in a bolt, hearing it clank around, never knowing when the fan is going to blast it back at me. And those bolts really smart when they hit you which makes the game all the more challenging.

Pretty soon we are in a frenzy, tossing in bolts and scampering like hell. Milt gets hit in the back with a nut I had tossed and falls to his knees where he is nailed in the wrist by a bolt he has just thrown. We are in tears laughing. I laugh so hard that I have to stop for a minute because my head hurts.

Milt likes to approach close to the scoop, lob in a bolt and then try to dodge it like a matador without moving his feet. I haven't had so much fun ever in my life. Finally there is one stove bolt left. Milt tosses it in and almost immediately it comes hurling out of the scoop, misses us both and then makes a THWUNK when it hits the wall behind us.

For the first time that afternoon we turn to look at the wall. It looks like the Luftwaffe has strafed Milt's bedroom. There is a chest-high, 5-foot wide band of destruction. The hundreds of tiny ceramic components have burst into colored powder marks on the wall sometimes leaving pieces of wire sticking out from the plaster. Embedded into the drywall at all angles, the stove bolts are really impressive. The walls are punctuated with dozens of deep, star-shaped dents from hurling nuts and the occasional washer sunk in on edge. This wasn't going to be covered up easily.

Then we look down at the floor. It is littered with thousands of broken, multi-colored ceramic pieces and a whole bunch of stove bolts, nuts and washers mixed into a fine plaster dust blanket. Considering our past history, this is a desperate moment.

So Milt slowly scans the room, the machine-gunned wall, the debris. He calibrates his odds of ever living through the day and says, "We better go to the Fiesta Room and have a hamburger." And true to the Rule of Life we walk out of the house and through the back gate into the alley.

ACKNOWLEDGMENTS

To Vicci Turner and Kara Swayne for publishing most of these stories on their excellent site AramcoExpats.com. An invaluable resource for the Aramco diaspora, it is a kind of *Sun & Flare* or *Arabian Sun* for the 21st century.

To Kathy Montgomery and Selena Maranjian for their nearly 15 years of flawless work operating Brat Chat - a lively forum for Aramco-Americans that originally hosted many of these stories with the added bonus of the comments and encouragements from its members. Thank you all.

And to Steve Furman, the son of my godfather Steve Furman Sr., the first American boy to return to post-War Dhahran, a genius story teller and my misguided idea of a role model to this day.

Tim Barger is the co-author with his father T.C. Barger of *Out in the Blue: Letters from Arabia 1937-1940* and the author of *Pamela's Song: Love, Loss, Rock & Roll*. More of his stories about growing up in Aramco during the Fifties and Sixties are at **ArabianSon.com**.

For more fine non-fiction books about Saudi Arabia in both print and digital form please visit our website at **SelwaDigital.com**.

You can browse our hardcover book catalog and view various galleries concerned with this ancient and fascinating country at **SelwaPress.com**.

All of our titles are available from Amazon.

Made in the USA
San Bernardino, CA
19 February 2014